The Cadence
of Excellence:

Key Habits of Effective Sales Managers

by
Matthew McDarby

Foreword

I have known Matt McDarby for a long time now and in many different guises — from sales rep to vice president of sales to entrepreneur — but one thing has always remained constant, and that is his absolute commitment to improving the profession of sales and driving tangible outcomes for customers.

When Matt became my VP of sales at Huthwaite, he introduced me to the idea of creating an "operating rhythm" within the sales organization and the need for sales managers to structure and drive this rhythm. While it made sense in theory, the idea that sales could have a steady rhythm seemed at odds with the frenetic reality most of us were used to.

Over time, Matt expanded on his ideas about how to manage and coach salespeople, and it became clear to me that he was indeed 100% correct. The sales manager who focuses on the early stages of the pipeline can significantly reduce the kind of chaos that often afflicts the later stages of the sales cycle, such as buyer misalignment, discounting, and poorly qualified opportunities that stall. In addition, he demonstrated the power of effective sales coaching and how that skill is, regrettably, not always understood and is taught even less.

In the intervening years, Matt and I have worked together occasionally on some customer engagements as well as writing a number of white papers and e-books largely focused on sales management and strategy. What always impressed me was that Matt continued to expand on his ideas and develop them and most important, field test them. It became obvious to me that these ideas needed to be codified and developed into a handbook so that the widest possible audience of sales professionals could learn about and implement them in their own sales organizations. This is why I am delighted to be writing the foreword to this much-needed body of work.

As I mentioned, all of Matt's ideas are field tested, so this is not a conceptual or theoretical book. I can attest to this because I have seen his ideas in action. I have witnessed the power of getting sales managers to focus on the early stages of the pipeline, learning how to create value for their salespeople, skillfully coaching them to greater levels of achievement, and, maybe most of all, being able to create the operating rhythm that can sustain this winning formula.

One final observation I feel compelled to share is that Matt has always been extremely practical in his approach. Whether it is a white paper, blog post, and now this comprehensive book, he always wants to make sure the reader comes away with something that can be easily understood and immediately implemented. *The Cadence of Excellence: Key Habits of Effective Sales Managers* is exactly that — an invaluable tool that we will all be using for years to come in our individual pursuits of sales excellence.

John Golden, Chief Strategy Officer
Pipeliner CRM, and former CEO of Huthwaite, Inc.

Introduction

The number one problem I hear from virtually every sales manager I interact with is, "I don't have enough time to do ALL the things that I need to do." As a result, some really important parts of their job are not done particularly well. Sales management can be a lonely and unforgiving job.

I realized roughly a decade ago while working as a client executive for one of the preeminent sales performance companies, Huthwaite (founded by noted behavioral researcher Neil Rackham), that the difference between being an excellent leader and being just average — or worse — depends largely on the choices one makes with his or her time. I realized that if someone were able to help sales managers make better choices with their time and effort, then that would have a huge impact on the performance of the whole sales organization.

I experienced this first-hand and learned invaluable lessons by observing great leaders in action. In 2010, I started United Sales Resources, and I have devoted the last seven years to helping sales managers — from frontline sales managers to chief sales officers —become dramatically more efficient and effective leaders.

The main premise behind my current business is that if you want to significantly improve the performance of your salesforce, focus on becoming a strong and effective sales manager by solving the "no time for important things" problem that I just described.

To be clear, this is not a book about time management. This is a book about the enormous impact your choices can have on your performance and on the performance of your entire team.

Consider for a moment the choices you make every day, month, or quarter about how you will apply your effort and focus. I break these tasks into two categories: inwardly focused tasks and outwardly focused tasks. Inwardly focused tasks are the tasks that are focused on improving, evolving, or changing your skills and performance as a sales manager, while outwardly focused tasks are the ones that are focused on helping your team's performance.

Inwardly focused tasks require self-discipline, diligence, and dedication. Establishing your operating rhythm and then determining what specific metrics you will pay attention to are good examples of inwardly focused tasks that have a direct impact on how you function as a leader.

Rhythm and metrics are my **how as a sales manager**, and if I don't master the **how**, the *what* (I am trying to achieve) has very little chance of occurring the way I hope it will. If you strike an appropriate rhythm with your team that places focus on important activities that relate directly to your desired business outcome, you are going to be better able to achieve the outcome. Strike a rhythm that places too much focus on activities that do not relate directly to your desired outcome, and you can expect a poor result.

Another way to think about operating rhythm is to think of it as a *cadence* — a flow or rhythm of events. Imagine musicians all deciding for themselves when to start a song and how to play it. It's a cacophony. (If you've ever been to an elementary school band class, you know what I'm talking about.) Now think of an orchestra led by a conductor who knows what she can expect out of each individual musician and each instrument and so she just provides guidance and instruction to make sure that everyone reaches his or her potential and comes together as a team to create a beautiful, harmonious outcome. That's a much better scenario, isn't it? Choosing a sales team's cadence is possibly the most important thing a manager can do. You are your sales team's conductor, and you determine if the outcome is cacophony or symphony.

How you lead and motivate your sales team or entire field force is also a function of choices you make each and every day. For instance, how do you go about planning conversations with your salespeople? Are you intentional about helping them see the value of approaching their job with excellence? What conclusions are you trying to help them draw? What questions are you asking? These outwardly focused tasks — tasks that directly relate to how you interact with and manage your team — are the other half of the equation.

I've used this framework of *inwardly* versus *outwardly* focused tasks as the guide for structuring this book. The first five chapters focus on things sales manager need to do for themselves, and the final five chapters focus on interactions with your team.

My hope for readers of this book is that they take control of the time available to them and choose excellence over mediocrity. Achieving sales leadership mastery requires that you make different choices than most sales managers do. What would it be like if you had greater control over and impact on your sales team's performance? What new opportunities would you be able to capture? What problems would you solve? What degree of personal growth would you experience? What about your people?

My challenge to you as you read this book is to identify the few, small, immediate changes you can make (just like the people featured in stories throughout the book did) that will have a massive impact for you and those you lead today and in the future.

I have included a simple worksheet at the end of the book to enable you to commit to changing in some small or perhaps in some significant ways after you finish this book. Committing to change in writing has a way of creating a sense of self-accountability, and I strongly recommend that you take the first step toward sales leadership excellence by putting your plan in writing.

Table of Contents

CHAPTER 1

Finding Your Operating Rhythm

An Inwardly Focused Task

I first met Jeff Lautenbach in 2007 when he was running a nearly $2 billion region within IBM Software Group. I was introduced to Jeff through my then-boss at Huthwaite, Brian Saltzman. Brian was a brilliant mentor and coach, and after he cracked the IBM Software Group account as a sales executive, I was tapped to take over managing the relationship when Brian was rightly promoted. I was thrilled to be involved in the IBM relationship, and my task was to figure out how we could build on the value that we had delivered so far to our client and develop new opportunities to sell our content and programs to them. By all accounts, Jeff was a very successful seller and sales leader at IBM, and we met during his fifteenth year with Big Blue.

IBM's sales organization was renowned for its disciplined cadence and strong adherence to a predictable rhythm of sales planning and execution that everyone, from the senior-most sales leader to the frontline sales managers and sales executives in the field, followed to a tee.

In 2007, IBM Software Group was operationally driven around large deals. It had a strong bias as a business toward large enterprise license agreements (ELAs). Jeff ran roughly half of the software sales organization in the United States at the time. IBM SWG had grown mostly through acquisition in the preceding years, and it continued to add brands and software products in an effort to expand what it had to offer to its large enterprise clients. As a point of reference, enterprise software companies like IBM, Microsoft, Oracle, etc. focused only 10% to 20% of their selling effort on selling to new logos.

But now, in order to meet the company's aggressive growth goals, the IBM SWG sales organization had to do something new. It had to find a way to exploit what it called the "white space" — the customers with whom it had little or no current presence or foothold.

As Jeff told me at the time, "We were great dealmakers, but we weren't very good at creating value. We had to better differentiate our solutions and create value for our customers by helping them to see things differently. We had to move from being ELA-focused financial/numbers sellers to provocative sellers of business value." Which is where Brian and I came in. We were meeting to discuss how to achieve that transformation. Our ultimate business objective was to inject value into IBM's relationships with its customers. But in order to do that, Jeff and every other member of the sales leadership team needed to coach their salespeople to enable the shift toward being provocative sellers of business value.

"I had to get a 1,200-person sales organization to approach coaching and leading their teams in a consistent and more effective way…particularly in our early-stage deals," Jeff said.

This was particularly challenging because IBM's cadence placed a great deal of emphasis on late-stage deals that were almost ready to close. At the end of each quarter, the group's focus would shift toward the deals that had reached the latest sales stages in which the close was imminent. In the last few weeks before a quarter's end, there was a heavy shift of resources, time, and focus to those late-stage deals. Deep discounts were offered to customers to incentivize them to act on ELAs enterprise license agreements before the end of a given quarter to ensure IBM's quarterly financial objectives were met.

This heavy shift toward late-stage deals came at the cost of progress that could have been made on opportunities that were earlier in their development. This created a vicious cycle in which IBM's sellers and sales managers spent little time creating compelling business value for customers because they had to focus on simply getting deals closed. It felt like an unbreakable cycle, and anyone who has worked in a sales organization that has a late-stage focus knows that it is extremely difficult to break.

Like essentially all other sales managers, IBM SWG's sales managers had little to no extra time to coach their salespeople any more than they already did — let alone learn a new way to coach them. Time was the main enemy of our plan to change their sales process.

This was when Jeff had his "transformational" moment. He realized that from the top of his organization down to frontline sales managers, their cadence would have to change. There was no way around it. But changing the cadence at an organization as wide and deep as IBM SWG is no small task. It would have been straight up impossible if Jeff had not carefully considered how to change his cadence (*internal task*) and then how to sell the new cadence to every member of his staff (*external task*). Put simply, he would have to help them all see the value of shifting their focus away from the normal, quarterly big deal/ELA rhythm they had been in for years and toward a new, early-stage and value-creation-focused operating system. "We needed to shift from a culture of reporting the news to a culture of making the news."

In Jeff's own words: "Managers had to make time for regular, brief, early-stage deal sessions. We would also do regular reviews of our competitive position (and win strategies) at key accounts, and they would incorporate a manager's whole team in a collaborative session. These sessions were hugely valuable, and they did not take much time." Group-based deal reviews put the focus on how IBM SWG would create business value and help customers.

The impact of this shift in focus was immediately apparent as success was attributed to specific wins with major customers. These wins entailed less discounting, and clients committed not because of quarterly end pressure but because there was compelling business value in it for them.

When the impact of this change was clear at the top line (revenue went up because more deals were won and those deals were, in fact, larger than they would have been otherwise), the lessons stuck and momentum grew quickly. What began as a small set of seemingly minor changes gained scale quickly, like a snowball rolling downhill, gaining size and speed. Other regions within the group took notice, and stories of big wins without quarter-end discounts and firefighting became lore.

While incremental changes in the group's cadence took place, my task was to help Jeff coach the sales managers to use their time with salespeople *asking questions* instead of *telling* their salespeople what their strategies should be. In addition to the basic discovery questions with which they were already comfortable, sales managers learned to ask questions with strategic intent. They asked questions like, "Why IBM, why now? If the customer does not solve this problem with us, what bad things will happen? What is the cost (to the customer) of waiting?"

Managers were expected to be on hand, often with Jeff or one of his third-line sales managers to observe, coach regularly, and demonstrate their effectiveness as coaches. One of the ways we managed the limited time (or reallocation of time) was that some of the time that would have previously been spent on late-stage, enterprise deals was refocused on early-stage deals that needed coaching in order to fully develop and to eventually land in the win column for IBM.

"We were learning together, and our reps were gaining traction," Jeff said. And so the case for a new cadence was made.

Over time, the organization's new cadence afforded Jeff and his sales leadership staff time to not only coach specific deals and to create value and insight for their salespeople but to address critical performance issues that existed in the ranks as well. After assessing each team member's performance according to certain key behaviors, sales managers in Jeff's region were asked to develop a plan for getting those who were evaluated as Low to Medium performers to a higher level of performance as soon as possible. They investigated the question together as a group: "How do we make sure we have time to develop those people who have potential to grow and produce more?"

The answer, once again, was to rely on the organization's focused and well-tuned cadence to ensure there was enough time to coach people who had the potential to develop and contribute more.

Speaking about the impact this experience had on his approach to leadership, Jeff shared, "It was really transformational for me." I will tell more of Jeff's present-day story later in the book, but suffice it to say that his story should be inspiring and instructive for every sales manager, regardless of tenure, industry, or capability.

One of the greatest challenges in any management position is knowing where to focus and how to avoid constant firefighting. In sales management, this is perhaps even more acute due to the inherently dynamic nature of sales. Under pressure to deliver revenue, sales leaders will often migrate toward the latter stages of the sales process, believing that closing deals is the best use of their time. But by doing so, they are implicitly endorsing poor selling practices. This is how ineffective sales leaders operate. Pace and activities are dictated by the *perceived opportunity* rather than a *conscious and measurable operating rhythm.*

This is a setup for chaos and an inability to effectively track behaviors and outcomes for future planning purposes. The longer you operate this way, the harder it becomes to identify what works and what doesn't for filling pipelines and closing deals.

Average to poorly performing managers tend to allow their team's operating rhythm to be dictated to them by external forces (e.g., the big boss, other departments, customers). When the big boss calls for an update to the forecast every day, the average manager turns his or her problem into a problem for the entire team. Rather than allowing his or her team to stay in rhythm (e.g., planning for upcoming calls, refining opportunity strategies, and doing things that relate directly to sales achieving its desired outcome), the sales manager asks his or her team to drop everything and update the forecast with the latest, blow-by-blow information. How likely is a team to succeed if it regularly has to divert time away from effective selling in favor of administrative work or reporting? What happens when other departments or customers disrupt the rhythm of planning, execution, review, and collaboration among a sales team? In short, the outcome is affected negatively, and the sales manager bears a large share of the responsibility for allowing his or her team to get out of rhythm and off task.

Excellent managers know how to influence their team's focus and direct its effort toward important things like planning, critical and strategic thinking, and highly effective execution simply by setting a specific, and consciously crafted, operating rhythm.

One quick way to tell the difference between a great manager and an average manager is by looking at his or her calendar to see if there is a predictable rhythm that includes time for planning, observation, coaching, and the other key activities we will delve into throughout this book. The ones who have a predictable rhythm will always be the ones who excel.

CHAPTER 2

Leading with Influence

An Inwardly Focused Task

For eighteen months, I served as Huthwaite's vice president of enterprise sales, and eventually I moved off the company's payroll and became a contractor. Several people in the organization, including the enterprise salespeople in my charge, knew that I was a contractor, reporting to the CEO of the company. Technically, I was not an officer of the company, so I didn't have the same kind of power over my team that an officer of the company would have, despite the fact that I was still part of the leadership team and leading one of the key branches of the organization that managed our largest, most strategically important customers.

As you might expect, a few members of the sales team played that fact to their advantage (and presumably to my disadvantage). Enterprise salespeople who knew their way around our internal systems and processes could exploit that knowledge to get pretty much whatever they wanted. If they didn't get the answer they wanted from me, they would go to my counterpart and play "Mommy" against "Daddy."A couple of my salespeople were bullies. They were tenured reps who were willing to steamroll or shame anyone who got in their way, including me. I knew that I had to get them to toe the line, but they acted and spoke a lot like adversaries, even when I was present. Though the company's strategy was clear as day, some members of my team went ahead as if we were still the same old company with the same old (unsustainable) strategy. Because they were the face to our customers, they had a great deal more control over the message being delivered to our enterprise customers than I did.

My mission was to get these salespeople to operate and sell according to the new company strategy, but because I couldn't simply command them to shape up or ship out, I had to find a way to influence their behavior in another way.

However, influencing how they approached situations so that their behavior matched more closely with what I wanted from them was very difficult because so much of what they did was out in the field and out of my view.

So I focused on only areas where I knew I could create some value for them, and I always had a plan for how I would approach conversations with the team. If there were certain conclusions I needed them to draw about our strategy or how to carry it out, then I would plan questions to open up the discussion, listen for and address any pushback, clarify, and eventually get the team to conclude that what I was asking them to do was really important not just for me but for them.

I also kept our focus as a team very narrow. When they met with me, it was usually about one of two or three things such as opportunity planning, call planning, or understanding the current status of early-stage opportunities in the pipeline. I told them flat-out, "If you remember only one thing from our work together, it will be that we focused on the early stages of the pipeline together and that I invested heavily into planning with you to ensure we get the outcomes we want." Eventually, they acquiesced (at least on the planning with me part), and the team exceeded its revenue goals in 2010 and in 2011.

Some sales managers, particularly those who are new to the role, believe their power lies in the ability to change their salespeople's behavior or their ability to implement strategy. But the reality is that this "power" is largely an illusion. Despite the fact that sales managers have supervisory relationships with salespeople, the salespeople actually have the balance of power because they are the ones working in the field, communicating with customers, and choosing (or not) to act in accordance with the prescribed strategy methods and norms, processes, tools, etc. A sales manager has the power to discipline or fire a salesperson for cause or based on poor performance. These episodic moments of power are nothing more than moments in time in the relationship between manager and seller. So much of the interaction and relationship between manager and seller are shaped not by power but by influence.

There is a difference between exerting power and having influence. With a mindset of guiding, supporting, and influencing your sales team's behavior, you will achieve a certain amount of power, but it is earned, not bestowed.

Thus, a fundamental challenge for a sales manager is to find a way to consistently influence his or her team's behavior without actually having much direct power — or control — over how their very human salespeople act.

A sales manager's influence comes down to how well he or she helps salespeople see new and different opportunities, identify and address problems in their approach, find new ways to get the outcome they are paid to achieve, and leverage available resources salespeople might not have known about.

This brings to mind a story about a current client of mine that is in the medical device business. Sales managers for that company have anywhere from eight to ten field salespeople in their charge, and their salespeople tend to be spread out over an area roughly the size of a couple of states — Maryland and Virginia, for example. Though they spend time with every salesperson in the regular course of their job, the sales managers do not have very much time with any one salesperson, and many of their field visits together involve joint calls on doctors and other hospital employees who influence the purchase of this company's devices. With so little time together in the field and so much time spent on joint selling, this company's sales managers have to thread the needle when it comes to influencing their salespeople's behavior. Coaching sessions must make an impact on salespeople's behavior each and every time, or valuable selling and management time is essentially wasted. The top sales managers — the ones who consistently deliver great sales results — maximize their time with salespeople by sticking to the discipline of planning and effective dialogue. Their average counterparts tend to *wing* coaching sessions, opting to tell rather than ask and allowing conversations to meander rather than come to a clear conclusion and a clear plan of attack.

I have a simple planning formula for sales managers who want to build a habit and a system that are based on influencing their salespeople virtually every day. This is the very same formula that I have encouraged sales managers that I coach to adopt, and they have done so with great and positive effect on their performance and on the value they are able to create for their salespeople.

The simple formula follows:

- **What conclusion(s) do I want this salesperson to draw?**
  - ° For example, are there gaps in the rep's selling strategy or opportunities that he or she is missing?
  - ° What does the salesperson need to think about differently?
- **What questions will I ask him or her to lead to that conclusion?**
  - ° What problems or opportunities do I need the rep to reflect on?
  - ° What assumptions do I need to challenge?
  - ° How will I help him or her develop a new or simply better approach to dealing with the situation at hand?
- **What action or commitment do I want the salesperson to take/make that represents some forward progress?**
  - ° What specific steps do I want the rep to take?
  - ° What other actions might the salesperson need to take?
  - ° How can I help the salesperson feel as though this plan is his or hers and not mine?

Questions, Conclusions, and *Actions* are the foundation of influence.

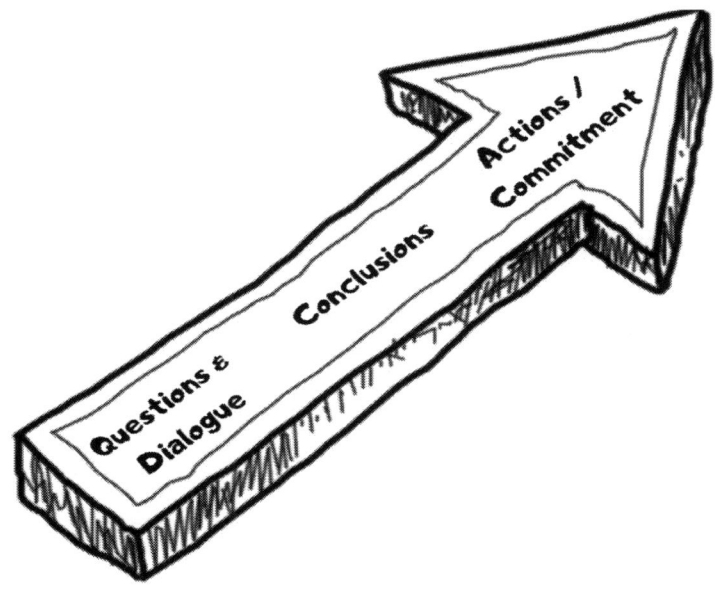

Consider the notion of "influence" in another context that we know well and can easily relate to. As professional salespeople, we know that our task when engaging with customers is to influence them to buy from us versus another source. We have the capability (meaning our own personal brain power and creativity but also the products, services, and resources we can make available) to solve problems or address opportunities for customers. We can choose to simply go out into the field and tell customers that we have the ability to address problems they don't yet recognize or opportunities they were missing out on, but for the most part, customers don't like being told anything, especially by salespeople.

Let's investigate that for a moment while we are pondering what it means to lead with influence. The reason our customers tend to place low value on what they are told is really quite simple. They are human beings, and human communication is bound by certain universal and timeless rules. Two quotes from very different times and contexts illustrate my point.

In the mid-1600s, French mathematician, physicist, inventor, writer, theologian, and all-around influential guy Blaise Pascal wrote, "People are generally better persuaded by the reasons which they have themselves discovered than by those which have come into the mind of others." Pascal had experienced the natural pushback and tendency of humans to disbelieve what they are told by others in favor of conclusions they had drawn on their own, no matter how strong the evidence might have been to the contrary.

Fast-forward about 350 years to the modern day, and you find virtually the same idea in the book, *Escaping the Price-Driven Sale* by my former colleagues Kevin Kearns and Tom Snyder. Kearns and Snyder wrote, "People value their own conclusions more than what they are told by others. People value what they request versus what is freely given to them."

If you've ever made a sales call on a customer and pitched a great new idea without first determining if the customer would find value in hearing about the idea, then you've experienced what Pascal, Kearns, Snyder, Rackham, and a veritable host of writers on the topic of sales excellence have written about before. If it isn't their idea, then prepare for pushback.

The likelihood of others doing what they are told to do (versus what they conclude on their own they should do) is very low. If you have been professionally trained as a salesperson, you might recognize a common thread running through all of the customer-focused, consultative, or value-oriented sales methodologies such as SPIN, Challenger, Solution Selling, etc. Though they each use slightly different language to do so, they all encourage sellers to plan and ask effective questions, to help customers arrive at new or different conclusions, and to propose some action that represents forward momentum toward a buying decision. The reason for that clear connection between all of those methodologies is simple: *Our ability to sell hinges on our ability to influence others' thinking.*

Now, compare the task of selling to coaching. As coaches, we have to help someone (i.e., sellers) arrive at new conclusions. Perhaps they are taking the wrong approach to an important meeting with a buyer, or they do not spend enough time planning, opting to fly by the seat of their pants without giving much consideration to the outcome or the impact on the relationship with a customer. Think of those sellers as buyers of new ideas that will help them achieve something they might not otherwise be able to achieve. How would you get them to accept your ideas, knowing about the human communication boundaries that exist and cannot simply be ignored?

How would you get them to come to new conclusions about their (currently ineffective) approach without telling them? How would you help them weigh the cost of taking the wrong approach compared to the potential payoff of taking a more effective approach?

Will you tell them what to do, or will you influence their behavior by helping them come to new conclusions on their own? Will you tell them to change, or will you create a state of awareness in which they realize they must change?

At this point, the choice is likely obvious. Just as it is in selling, our ability to influence our salespeople boils down to how well we are able to help them reach new and different conclusions about their own performance. We do this by planning — Conclusions, Questions, and Actions.

Selling is about influence, and coaching is about influence. Therefore, **coaching is a great deal like selling**. In fact, I will go one step further to say that **coaching is selling**.

If you are finding it more difficult than ever to influence the behavior of your salespeople and customers, then perhaps it is time to consider a change in your approach to influencing and selling internally. Are you working at your craft as an influencer and coach as much as you once did on your skills as a seller? If not, then why not? If not now, when will you do so?

CHAPTER 3

Using Data and Metrics to Guide Sales

An Inwardly Focused Task

Dennis Currens and Lance Strefling each have several decades in the food business, the last couple of decades with Maplehurst Bakeries serving the needs of in-store bakeries at major retailers throughout the U.S. and Canada. I came to know them both in 2011, and my role was to serve as their coach and sales leadership advisor during a period of dramatic growth. The company has grown through acquisition, consolidation, and organic new sales growth, nearly doubling in revenues and staff headcount.

Dennis and Lance were each responsible for revenue targets measured in the hundreds of millions of dollars, and they shared responsibility for achieving some rather aggressive growth goals. Despite the daunting numbers for which they were responsible, they turned in an incredible performance over the course of a five-year period in which the company achieved record sales growth each and every year.

When they and their respective teams first set out on the big growth initiative, they committed to a different approach to selling, one that was predicated and built upon their ability to create value for customers based on how they sold. They sell commodity items, but they had to take an approach to selling that pre-empted the commoditization of the ways in which they delivered their products. They had to better understand their clients' visions of success, and they had to demonstrate how Maplehurst would help clients achieve their particular vision.

"Most companies just go about selling what they make. That was what we did in the past," Dennis explained. "We weren't looking forward enough or planning effectively," and this was a significant barrier to the salesforce succeeding at taking away business from competitors and identifying and winning new opportunities.

"We sometimes chased the wrong priorities," he added. "When we had information or data to use, we had trouble identifying the right issues for our customers." This was mainly because their teams made assumptions about the data without discussing and validating the issues or opportunities suggested by the data with their customers. And so, Dennis and Lance had to change the way the sales organization used information and the tools at its disposal to better identify and pursue the right opportunities.

Lance shared, "We had a long way to go to understand how to use data effectively internally and also how to use it with our customers."

Before they made a commitment to using data to guide their value-creation effort, Dennis said, "we didn't have the clearest view of where we were, so we were unclear about where we needed to go." Every account or opportunity planning discussion was more complicated and less effective than it needed to be.

One of the key initiatives that we worked on together was to refine the group's practices and interpretation of data that was available in its customer relationship management (CRM) software, Salesforce.com. On top of the company's use of Salesforce, another application called Dealmaker laid over the Salesforce database, offering a simple but detailed value of everything from the state of the entire business pipeline down to the health and probability of individual opportunities. Dennis, Lance, and I worked on developing the ability to quickly assess data as it was presented in a Dealmaker visual report and quickly converting that into a value-creating dialogue with a salesperson.

"My job as a leader became easier when we rallied together around some piece of information or some bit of customer data, even if it was incomplete data," Dennis said. "It gave us a path to where we wanted to go" and illuminated where they wanted to take the buyer. "We were much clearer about what it would take to create value for the customer and what we needed to do together to help each other."

There are clearly times when Dennis and Lance need a salesperson from their respective teams to focus on value, ask better questions, and more fully clarify or validate what matters to the customer. There are also scenarios in which the buying decision will be made based solely on price, and the data on hand for each and every opportunity in the pipeline tells a clear story about which approach is appropriate. Do we create value in this opportunity, or do we make the process of buying as simple as possible and keep costs low to win the business? Dennis and Lance have learned how to use data to lead the sales team to approach each opportunity in the most effective and/or efficient way.

For every business, there is a time to emphasize efficiency (i.e., sales activities in high numbers) and a time to emphasize effectiveness (i.e., getting good sales outcomes), but those two things are rarely if ever needed in equal proportion at the same time.

The sales manager's job is to strike the right balance between efficiency and effectiveness based on his or her business needs at the time. The question is how.

First, there is the task of identifying where the sales effort might be out of balance. Below are two quick examples to help illustrate the point:

The Efficiency Play — Dan is a sales manager with a small team of sellers in a services sales organization. All of his sellers are strong in terms of their domain expertise and business acumen in the industry they serve. They are very credible and effective when in front of customers, and the company's strong reputation in its space leads to a relatively high sales conversion rate. In short, their sellers are very effective. Dan notices while looking at a pipeline report that the overall, gross value of his team's new business pipeline is short of the total revenue goal that has been assigned to it. He knows he has a problem.

Dan knows that in order to close the gap between his team's current pipeline value and the revenue goal, the sellers will need to have far more opportunities in the pipeline than they do currently. In order to identify and develop the kinds of opportunities that belong in the pipeline, the sales team will have to make a great deal more touches on their target prospects and customers. Dan decides to set a new activity goal for every member of his team, requiring each seller to increase calls and first meetings with prospective customers with an eye toward increasing the number of opportunities and eventually increasing the total gross revenue in the team's pipeline. This is an efficiency play.

The Effectiveness Play — Mary is a sales manager from a different services firm across town from Dan. Her team of sellers is somewhat less tenured than Dan's team, but they hold their own competitively. The firm has grown aggressively over the last several years, landing more new clients than most other firms in the region have been able to do. The sales team has a reputation in the local market as being hustlers who work very hard.

Mary notices one day while reviewing her team's pipeline report that the overall gross value of the team's revenue pipeline is high — well above its goal for the revenue — but she does a calculation of the economic, weighted value of the pipeline and is immediately concerned. Mary has a problem.

Mary knows that in order to increase the economic, weighted value of her pipeline, she has to do something about the root problem. Why does the team have such a large gross revenue pipeline but show so little in terms of economic value? The answer appears in the middle to late stages of her team's pipeline, where she notices that a very large number of the team's deals either lag or fall out completely. All of that initial, gross value that the team works to build into the pipeline seems to be falling out about halfway through the pipeline. Mary knows that in order to address this issue, the team will have to do a better job of developing opportunities and creating value for prospective customers so opportunities stop dying on the vine and instead reach full fruit.

Mary decides to sit the sellers down to talk about how they will work together to be more effective and focused on creating value for their customers in order to strengthen the pipeline. They will devote more time together to planning and to being generally more thoughtful about how they position themselves in light of customer needs and also with respect to competitive options. This is an effectiveness play.

Implied in the *Effectiveness Play* and the *Efficiency Play* is the need for data that informs a sales manager's decision-making. The examples that I offered in these stories of Dan and Mary and also Lance and Dennis all hinge on a sales manager's ability to use data to diagnose where problems or opportunities lie in the quest for great sales results. In the 2000s and 2010s (to date), that data typically came from CRM software and/or plug-ins that pulled specific data to create management dashboards and easy planning tools. As technology advances, the sources of data and how that data and information about customers, opportunities, and specific sales activities are used will continue to evolve. What will a data- and information-driven approach to sales leadership look like in the near and foreseeable future?

A new landscape of discovery tools guided by machine learning or artificial intelligence (AI) has arisen recently in the world of professional sales and sales enablement. Developments in the fields of data management, machine learning, and management user interfaces have converged to create a powerful new class of tools that are meant to deliver insight into the performance of entire sales teams and also individual territories, reps, and specific opportunities. As is often the case with emerging technologies, the promise of making the complex task of diagnosing human performance in sales as easy as the touch of a button is at least somewhat overstated. The reality is that these new tools such as Gong, Chorus, Refract, Rehearsal, and ExecVision derive and deliver maximum value when placed in the hands of a thoughtful diagnostician. By "thoughtful diagnostician," I am not necessarily referring to an expert in data science or in technology but to someone with intellectual curiosity, some basic business sense, and the willingness to ask questions like the following:

- Why? What leads to or contributes to what this data suggests?
- How do we know this is true?
- What does this information appear to indicate?
- How can we validate what this data is telling us?

I recently started a working relationship with Mark Ackers and Kevin Beales from Refract, a conversation intelligence software company based in the UK. The Refract toolset makes it possible to record, review, and give feedback on the execution of real-world sales calls, practice role plays, and other recorded practice scenarios in an asynchronous way. In other words, they solve the problem of managers being unable to observe their salespeople in lots of different types of scenarios because of distance, time, conflicts, cost, etc. If a sales manager cannot observe how a salesperson executes essential tasks of the job, then a sales manager cannot give coaching and constructive feedback.

The Refract platform and other conversation intelligence platforms like it represent a breakthrough approach to an age-old problem, and solutions like this didn't even exist just a few years ago. The economy of effort and great efficiency that this platform offers for a coach who seeks to develop the skills of a far-flung team of various levels of sales capability is a huge advantage.

Kevin Beales will be one of the first people to dispel false claims about the impact of sales conversation intelligence platforms and to clarify their actual value. "Refract's strategy is to develop technology that provides insight into what separates top performers from others." As Kevin puts it, conversation intelligence technology will "give us great insights into how people are performing behind closed doors."

Implied in that statement is the idea that salespeople somehow perform differently when their sales managers are sitting with them, observing how they interact with customers, how they plan and execute, and so forth. Do salespeople sometimes put on an act for us sales managers, behaving in an apparently optimal way when we are watching only to behave in a suboptimal way when we aren't watching? The sad truth is yes, some salespeople put on their best behavior only when the boss is watching. But our task as sales leaders is to help salespeople perform each and every day like they do on their best days.

That is why Refract's platform and other tools that serve up insights on the whole of a salesperson's effort are so potentially valuable to a sales leader today. Observing how salespeople handle internal tasks and external, client-facing tasks is a crucial building block to a high-performance, coaching-friendly culture. We can derive insights and come to our own conclusions about what might be preventing a salesperson from reaching his or her full potential by looking at data, but to be clear, the data alone does not get the job done.

While attempts are being made as I write this book to develop insights that span hundreds of thousands of sales calls across the globe to identify the perfect discovery call, for example, the reality is that every sales organization will have its own correct recipe for delivering great results. As Kevin from Refract explains, "If you compare datasets between two very similar companies, you will find loads of difference." In other words, there is never going to be a simple formula for success that data combined with AI will be able to discover and deliver to sales organizations universally. Instead, the real-world value equation for sales performance data and AI tools will look something like this:

DATA x CRITICAL THINKING = VALUE

The ultimate VALUE of DATA rendered from CRM and sales intelligence platforms to an organization is multiplied by the critical and contextual THINKING of a sales manager.

How do you use data and whatever sales intelligence is available to you right now? Do you only use sales data to "manage" your people's performance, or do you use data to plan smart questions about the root causes of poor performance? Do you use technology in any way to identify opportunities for your people or your whole team to improve?

If not, then why not? What will happen if your competitors are smarter and better informed about the behaviors that will lead to better sales outcomes?

CHAPTER 4

Aligning Sales with Go-To-Market

An Inwardly Focused Task

I had the opportunity to work with and eventually report to John Golden from the time that he joined Huthwaite as CEO in August 2008 until I ended my official role at Huthwaite two-and-a-half years later. When John joined the company, the salesforce was thoroughly fatigued and at times confused about who we were, who we were trying to be, and whether we were going to survive.

John tells a story about one of his first client meetings as CEO. "They told me, 'We love your stuff. Don't know what else you do, but you are really hard to do business with.'" That message stuck with John, and it drove a few important changes that began to take hold just a few months after his arrival.

Were we a training company? A consulting company? Something else that defied description? In short, John concluded that we were trying to be too clever. "It's like the line from the movie, *This is Spinal Tap*: there is a 'fine line between stupid and clever.' If we weren't clear about who we were, how could customers be clear?"

The evidence of our lack of clarity could be found not only in client meetings but in our sales pipeline. In short, we were unfocused. We had a wide variety of opportunities that carried descriptions like *value creation strategy* and *process consulting*, but the reality was that we had very few resources that could do that sort of work reliably and effectively. I was personally as guilty as anyone else, as a global account director with all sorts of consulting gigs piling up in my pipeline.

We had to focus, and that meant we had to make choices. Further, we had to un-choose other things. At Huthwaite, that meant we had to stop approaching every engagement as a blue sky or a green field, and instead, we needed to focus on being really good at what we really did. In this way, we would be able to close the gap between what we promised and what we were able to deliver.

An opportunity came for me to move up in the ranks, and I became Huthwaite's vice president of enterprise sales. I reported directly to John and immediately plugged in with his effort to help the sales team better align itself with the company's clearer go-to-market strategy and message.

As a result of the hard choices we made and the clarity with which the salesforce was able to approach clients, we were successful at not only turning the business around after the 2009 economic downturn, but the company's sales reached record levels in 2011, 2012, and 2013. Clients had a clearer and more accurate expectation of what we were good at, and we were better at delivering our message to them.

Aligning sales with the go-to-market led to an unexpected outcome for some of us salespeople. Clients began to develop an appetite to learn more about what we had to offer, and we had a new problem (or opportunity) to address. We had clients coming to us proactively and rehiring and expanding their relationships with us, which was a rare phenomenon historically. We found that the trust we were able to build by sticking to our core and the value we were able to create through insights and creativity strengthened our relationships with clients in a way that we could not have imagined.

Eventually, a sales organization will have the chance to share more of its capabilities, and it will find clients more receptive based on the trust it has built and the value the company has delivered. Conversely, a salesforce that develops and focuses its time on opportunities that fall outside the company's core capabilities and require a great deal of gyration and contortion to deliver will ultimately collapse upon itself.

Sales managers operate in the zone where strategy meets tactics. On a daily basis, they have the unenviable task of balancing the demands of the executive team ("we need growth, sell more"), the demands of customers ("help us solve problems, help us capture opportunities"), and the demands of their salespeople ("help us make our quota and reach our personal, financial objectives"). I call this balance unenviable because at any given time, one, two, or all three of those demands appear to be in conflict.

Following is an illustration of what I mean: Newco is a player in the highly competitive sales enablement software-as-a-service market, and Jane is an enterprise sales manager. Jane's chief sales officer and the rest of the senior leadership team have aggressive revenue growth goals for the current and next fiscal years. Jane is told that in no uncertain terms, her future with the company depends on her enterprise sales team meeting or exceeding their financial objectives for each of the next six quarters. The company's solutions are moderately priced, but they have some competitive obstacles to overcome. A lack of mature products and features in the company's online suite means it can only compete for certain types of business, even though it is considered alongside several other, established players that have broader products and integration capability. Newco is capable of competing and winning in certain scenarios, and there are other scenarios where its lack of capability or referenceable clients would make it difficult or impossible to compete.

Jane's team of enterprise sellers is highly compensated, and each member of the team carries a multimillion-dollar quota. In the hunt for big numbers, Jane's salespeople have developed the habit of pursuing a lot of opportunities. Their former sales manager required them to pursue a total pipeline value of three to four times their annual revenue quota, meaning they would have to find and maintain roughly $6 million to $8 million or more gross revenue in their pipeline at any time. That remains an unwritten rule, and senior leadership gets very impatient with the salesforce when the gross value of the pipeline drops below an acceptable level. Average deal sizes range from $150,000 to $250,000 per year, so each salesperson needs to have approximately forty active opportunities in his or her pipeline at any given time to meet the pipeline value expectation.

Jane also has her own objectives. She is not only responsible for a $40 million-plus quota, but she also has performance bonuses tied to profitability and to each salesperson on her team achieving quota. The problem in a nutshell is that Jane is under massive pressure from senior leadership to deliver big numbers in a market where it is tough to compete for every deal. Her salespeople are also feeling the pressure to maintain a hefty pipeline, and they need to stay at or ahead of their financial objectives throughout the year to keep the dogs at bay. Customers apply their own special brand of pressure, demanding discounts or special, unreasonable terms that create a great deal of risk for Newco.

How does Jane keep senior leadership, the sales team, customers, and herself satisfied? How can she take these seemingly competitive and exclusive demands and find a way to satisfy them? She can drive her salespeople like sled dogs until they collapse. She can blow sunshine in the general direction of her senior leadership team, letting them know everything is A-OK. She can allow her team to show a pipeline full of (garbage) deals that are unlikely to close and go in Newco's favor. She can also allow her sales team to pursue and respond to large tenders and requests for proposals, using valuable company resources and time. After all, you have to be *in it to win it.*

Or she can be highly disciplined and discerning about the opportunities that her team pursues. She can seek, find, and be able to repeat the answers to the following questions:

- What are we good at?
- What do we really want to be known for as a company?
- How do we stuff our pipeline with the right types of opportunities?
- What are the right types of opportunities in the first place?
- What do we do when the wrong types of opportunities happen along?

The sales manager has to be able to look at the pipeline with the team and say let's do this, let's not do this, etc. Communicating this information and helping your team to align with the plan can often require finesse.

Many organizations are having conversations about how sales and marketing departments can collaborate to produce better, more effective collateral and tools for the company. Those are good conversations to be having; however, there is a fundamental step that needs to take place first, and that is for the leaders of the company — whether they are executives or frontline sales managers — to sit down with marketing and other relevant groups to review the company's go-to-market (GTM) strategy. This is because the company's GTM should be the source from which sales, marketing, and every other function in the company draw their understanding about the value proposition, how the products/services are positioned, and most important, who their target customers are and what common characteristics they share. The sales manager plays a pivotal role because he or she is ultimately the point at which strategy directly intersects with the market.

In order for a company to consistently deliver on its promises of service and quality to customers, the sales organization must focus on selling what the company is actually good at delivering. This sets us up for future sales, longer-lasting customer relationships, and sustainable growth.

Effective sales managers use the GTM strategy as the foundation for a deliberate and informed decision-making process. It forms the basis of their sales strategy, including:
- Working with each of their salespeople to target the right customer
- Ensuring that prospecting plans are leveraging the right value proposition, messaging, and positioning
- Properly qualifying opportunities early in the sales cycles to ensure they meet the right target customer profile
- Collaborating with support and implementation teams to appropriately resource and support the right opportunities

But salespeople like to sell and are more inclined to chase any deal that looks promising (or will provide a commission or get them to sales goals), even if it's not directly aligned with the company's core competencies or capacity to deliver. If that was true at Huthwaite (where we sold sales effectiveness), then it is most certainly true in lots of other places. The challenge for the sales manager then is to find a way to redirect or guide the salespeople in line with the organization's strategy, without reducing motivation or drive within those salespeople.

Sales managers are responsible for ensuring that salespeople are working on the right opportunities with the right types of customers. In this way, they are the key enablers of a company's strategy. In Neil Rackham's words, "Sales managers play the pivotal role." My interpretations of Rackham's words are that we sales managers had better be able to balance the strategic direction of the company (i.e., the GTM) with the tactical pursuits of salespeople.

We sales managers have the pivotal role, and we also have a challenging and unenviable role as well. The challenge, simply described, is to remain laser-focused on helping our salespeople pursue and develop the right opportunities with the right types of customers, all the while keeping them motivated and fully bought into the strategy.

What makes this so difficult? Surely keeping salespeople motivated is just a matter of tapping into what matters most to them personally — correct? I wish it were that simple. We salespeople are generally optimistic, persistent, and at times aggressive, and we love to win. Those are some of the traits that made us such a great match for the profession of selling in the first place.

The fact that salespeople typically have these traits also leads to one of the great challenges to keeping a sales team well focused and aligned with the company's GTM. The subtext of keeping in alignment with a company's GTM emphasizes the need to win not *every* deal but to win the *right* deals. Quite literally, this will mean walking away from the wrong opportunities and the wrong customers, which might seem in conflict with other messaging we deliver at times about the need to continually fill and maintain a strong sales pipeline. It might also be in conflict with the aggressive pipeline objectives we might be giving our salespeople.

How can we avoid sending conflicting messages to our salespeople? How can we tell them in one breath about the need for a healthy, robust pipeline and in the very next breath tell them about the need for diligence in qualifying opportunities out of the pipeline if they are not a good fit? In short, we sales managers must be more thoughtful about the pipeline objectives we set and how we describe them to our people going forward. Following is an example to illustrate my point, using a fictional though not terribly unrealistic rep we'll call Jack.

Jack is an average sales performer who works hard to maintain a sizable pipeline of new business. He is in his second year with the company. His original hiring manager, who has since left the company, set a 3X revenue pipeline objective for Jack, meaning Jack's goal was to maintain a total revenue pipeline value equal to three times his annual quota. Jack succeeded at reaching his 3X revenue goal, but upon deeper review, you (his new sales manager) notice that Jack has several large "custom engagement" opportunities in his pipeline. Without those custom engagements factored into his total revenue pipeline, Jack would be several hundred thousand dollars shy of achieving his pipeline revenue objective.

Knowing that your company historically struggles with "custom engagements," you grow concerned about the reality and likelihood of Jack's territory delivering a sufficient amount of revenue this year. He does not appear to have enough of the right types of opportunities in his pipeline to have a realistic chance of delivering his number. Do you:

(A) Change Jack's pipeline revenue objective to make it easier for him to achieve, hence avoiding the problem of demotivating him?

(B) Tell Jack to strip out the opportunities that are not aligned with the company's capabilities and GTM right now, his motivation be damned?

(C) Some combination of A and B?

(D) Discuss with him the impact of pursuing the wrong types of opportunities — on trust, profit, value of the deal, etc.?

(E) Discuss with him the potential payoff associated with focusing on the right deals with the right customers, showing him the likely, positive impact that will have on his ability to pursue not only new business but repeat business?

If you are reading these options and thinking maybe the answer is (C) or possibly it is some combination of (D) and (E), then I will let you off the hook. The real answer is: It depends. It depends on whether the salesperson in question is a pragmatist or a realist, a can-do type or a woe-is-me type, a numbers-driven person or a gut-feel type of person. This is yet another case where your critical thinking as a sales leader will make all the difference.

Considering the potential conflict between keeping your team members aligned with the GTM and maintaining their motivation to achieve aggressive pipeline objectives, there are some important and situation-specific questions you will have to consider before you go forward.

(1) How can I help my salespeople see the value of staying focused on the right deals?

(2) How can I help them see how much of a drain on time and resources the wrong deals can be?

(3) What supporting data or information can I share with them (e.g., historical win/loss reports) that illustrates our success rate on the right deals versus our success rate with the wrong types of deals?

CHAPTER 5

Focusing on Creating Maximum Value for Your Team

An Outwardly Focused Task

In business-to-business and particularly in complex sales (multiple buyers, multiple calls, addressing an important business problem or opportunity), the focus for many sales organizations is on value creation. Put a different way, many salesforces today are working to find a way to compete based on criteria other than price, so they seek to emphasize in some way the additional value of what they and their companies provide.

The first, best illustration of this challenge and opportunity for salesforces can be found in the book *Rethinking the Sales Force*, by John DeVincentis and Neil Rackham. DeVincentis and Rackham were far ahead of the market when they challenged the traditional notions of value and competitive differentiation in 1999. It took roughly a decade for many B2B sales organizations to start adapting to the reality that Rackham and DeVincentis illustrated in *Rethinking*.

A great deal has changed for B2B sales organizations since 1999, but one thing has not changed: Salesforces must continue to adapt to the changing demands and behavior of buyers. Modern sales organizations cannot achieve competitive differentiation simply by communicating the features and advantages of the products and services that they sell. You must understand how to create value for customers and know that it has everything to do with *how* you sell versus *what* you sell.

The big challenge nowadays is how to build a value-creating salesforce that can continually adapt to the constant and rapid changes going on in the marketplace around you. In early 2015, I set out to revisit the questions that Rackham and DeVincentis asked of buyers some sixteen years earlier, and the answers provide insight not only into what buyers value today but also what it takes for a sales leader to create maximum value for his or her team.

I asked roughly 800 people, recent buyers of products and services who had several equivalent options to choose from at the time of purchase, two questions:

1. In the last two years, have you made a significant purchase of a product or service from a supplier that was not the lowest price provider for that product or service?

2. If your answer was "Yes," what was the number one reason you chose to do business with that supplier?

The premise behind our questions was simply that if people had chosen to buy from a supplier that did not offer the lowest price, then there must have been some reason for them to do so. The buyers must have found some "value" associated with doing business with that supplier that justified paying more than they had to pay.

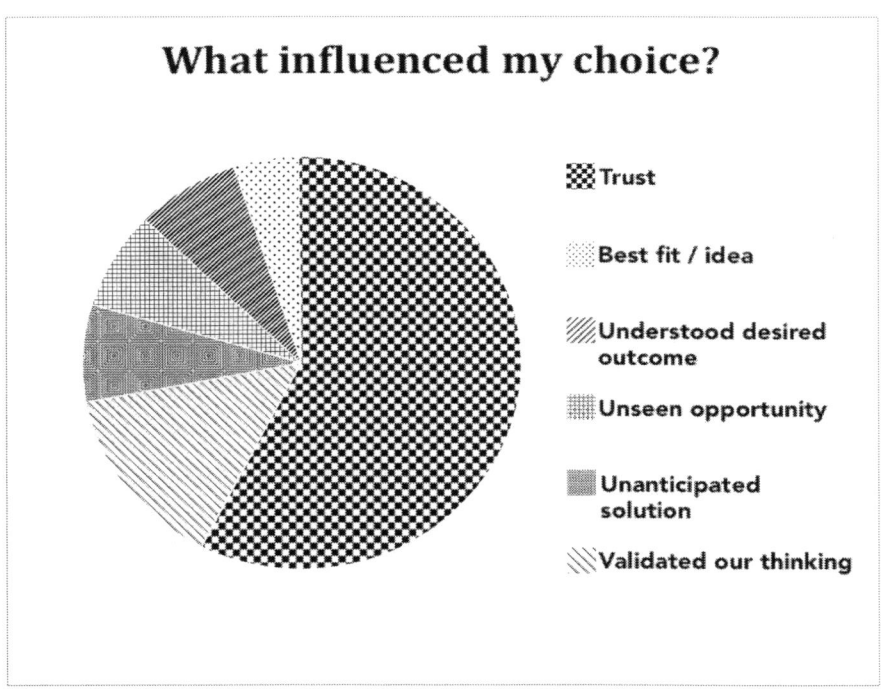

Perhaps not surprisingly, approximately 43% said that they had not purchased a single product or service from someone other than the lowest price provider in the last two years. I spared that price-driven group of buyers from answering the second question. The remaining 57% of respondents gave us the following as their top reasons for choosing to pay more than they needed to:

Slightly more than half of the respondents said they simply trusted the seller more than any other option. Despite a lower-priced option being available, they chose to purchase based primarily on trust. How is that instructive for a sales manager? Salespeople aren't paying for your services as a sales manager the same way a buyer pays for a product or service from a seller. There might be a parallel, however, that we need to consider. In what currency do salespeople and sales managers trade together? In short, I think the currency that passes back and forth between seller and sales manager is time.

If we ask our sellers to work with us planning their important sales calls, we are asking for some of their time. If a seller reaches out to his or her sales manager and asks for feedback on a proposal that is due to the customer in a few days, he or she is asking for some of the manager's time. How can we earn more of that ever important currency from each other? Based on my research, it appears the first, best thing we can do is build trust.

Consider two simple questions right now about you and your team:
- What am I doing to build trust with my people and vice versa?
- What am I doing to erode trust with my people and vice versa?

The remaining answers to my question about value suggest some other concrete actions we must consider taking if we plan to create value for our salespeople. If we expect them to offer the best idea/best fit solutions to customers, then we have to demonstrate that same capability in our interactions with them. In a sales transaction, that starts with listening to and understanding the other party's desired outcome. As a sales manager, are you focused on your desired outcome alone, or are you focused on helping your salespeople achieve their desired outcome? In the end, shouldn't you and your salespeople work together to identify a shared vision of success? If so, I submit that will be a more valuable use of your time compared to working separately to achieve two disparate versions of success.

Once you've done that, are you helping salespeople see problems or opportunities they otherwise would not recognize (the next few drivers of value that buyers identified in my survey)? How are you doing that? When are you doing that?

If a sales manager wants her salespeople to be able to create value by building trust, helping customers see problems or opportunities they otherwise would not recognize, being thoughtful, thinking strategically, and planning and executing with excellence, then *she must also model that same behavior.* There is no surer way to reinforce the wrong sales behavior than for a sales manager to talk about excellence but demonstrate mediocrity.

Effective sales managers spend their time at the beginning or the planning end of the sales cycle, which sets their teams up for success. Ineffective managers parachute in at the end to make sure the deal closes, which sets their teams up for long-term failure. This type of manager operates under the belief that there was no effective management during the earlier phases of the sales cycle (perhaps because they didn't guide their team in planning). But a manager who focuses on planning, coaching, and supporting her team during the early stages of a sales cycle is rarely needed to swoop in at the end. Instead, she can spend her time on things like making sure the pipeline is fully stocked and her salespeople are ready to go. When a sales manager has executed a comprehensive and effective early-stage focus, combined with the other management elements we're talking about in this book, the end of the sales cycle should be easily handled by the salesperson.

For example, if the sales manager has done a less than rigorous exploration of the customer's needs with the salesperson, then the result might be that the salesperson moves forward with a strategy based on false assumptions. An effective sales manager would coach the salesperson and send him or her back to do additional discovery work with the prospect, before allowing the opportunity to progress. The ineffective sales manager, likely busy firefighting late-stage opportunities, is more likely to decide that he will focus on the opportunity when it is a little further into the sales process and take at face value the assumptions being made. This almost guarantees that the sales manager will indeed be interacting with the opportunity later in the sales cycle as he tries to rescue a clearly misaligned customer.

Further, this type of management leads to a sales culture of shortcuts and bad selling habits that result in the early stages of the pipeline being stuffed with ill-qualified opportunities. This in turn wastes valuable resources, inflates the pipeline, and sends win/loss rations into a spiral. It becomes the classic numbers game. The sales manager is now so reliant on that smaller number of opportunities that make it to the latter stages of the pipeline that they have to invest all of their time there. This is where discounting rears its ugly head, sweeteners are thrown in, or last-minute customizations are promised, all of which are compensating for the lack of rigor and oversight earlier in the process.

It's a cycle that can be nearly impossible to break, unless sales managers are committed to changing the entire culture and operating method for themselves as well as their teams.

Effective sales managers understand that while there will always be times when their help is required with late-stage opportunities, their real job is to focus on appropriate prep work at the early stages so that these times are kept to a minimum. Stated another way, effective sales managers have an early-stage focus as a method for empowering their salespeople to achieve success.

When the sales manager has an early-stage focus, one of the biggest areas of impact is in opportunity selection. Every new opportunity that either is uncovered by a salesperson or comes into the lead queue by another route is immediately scrutinized by the sales manager to see how many of the characteristics of the ideal customer/opportunity it appears to have. This fills the pipeline with opportunities that are winnable.

When a sales manager has a set cadence that involves this kind of planning and attention to creating viable opportunities, it achieves two important objectives. First, it keeps the front end of the pipeline lean and uncluttered by speculative (long-shot) opportunities. Second, it teaches salespeople that they need to qualify opportunities more rigorously before they introduce them for review by the sales manager. Eventually, as salespeople contribute better qualified prospects, it reduces the workload and level of oversight required by the sales manager, freeing her up for other high-value activities such as coaching and mentoring.

CHAPTER 6

Building and Sustaining a Winning Team

An Outwardly Focused Task

When I first met Randy Majors, he was serving as a vice president of sales for the Americas and for global major accounts at Platts, a business unit within what was then known as the McGraw-Hill Business Information Group (or B.I.G.). For the first five years of our working relationship, I worked with Randy and his counterparts on the B.I.G. Sales Excellence Council until a major restructuring of the business broke up the group. After that restructuring, our working relationship continued for six more years during which Randy became the VP Global Sales, Marketing and Client Services for Platts, leading a sales team of roughly 200 salespeople and sales managers.

As the global head of sales, Randy was given the task of doubling the business's revenue in five years. Platts had grown significantly up to the time of his promotion by focusing primarily on providing its information services to one main commodity area: oil. In order to successfully grow the business and double revenue in just a few years, the Platts sales organization would have to find new ways to operate, sell, and create value for customers who did business in commodity areas such as metals and sugar production.

Selling in a value-creating way would be particularly difficult in commodity areas in which the Platts sales organization was unaccustomed. Without understanding the business issues and opportunities facing a metals firm, for example, the salesperson would struggle to create insight and value for a potential client in that industry. The organization would not succeed at establishing new clients, grabbing new market share, or doubling revenue. Platts sales needed to "truly add value" in every commodity area and in every interaction with clients.

In addition to making significant investments in training and tools for the sales organization, Randy and his team needed to focus on talent development. In other words, they had to make sure they had the most effective sales talent possible to carry out the strategy in the field, or the organization would not achieve its growth and financial goals.

The only thing more difficult than finding and retaining great sales talent is finding and retaining great sales management talent. Randy's focus on talent development and a few, key operating principles enabled his highly capable sales leadership team to stay intact (for the most part) for a period of roughly six to seven years. Maintaining a strong sales management team became possible because, according to Randy, he and his team focused on the following:

- We were open with each other, and we had candid debates.
- Once we made a decision, we spoke with one voice.
- The ground rules for decision-making were very clear.
- And ultimately, we held together as a sales leadership team because we were so well-aligned on what we needed to do and how we needed to do it.

They also gave people the opportunity to develop themselves, meaning they needed to take the initiative and use the resources available in a proactive way to develop themselves. People who weren't willing or able to do that would not be a good fit.

Platts succeeded at doubling its revenue ahead of schedule, and the global sales organization — from Randy down to second- and first-line managers and the field sales team — grew continually, adding new talent and delivering consistent growth year over year for a period of five years.

Finding winners who fit in your environment and who can become long-term sales success stories is extremely difficult. Knowing what and who to look for is a bit of a mystery to many sales managers, and managers should seek help in this process. I have personally worked with internal and external recruiters with great success. I also ran a small software sales recruiting business before joining Huthwaite, and

I have learned that there are a few things you can look for to help identify strong salespeople. My short list of characteristics of quality sales hires includes the following:

Resiliency — There is nothing worse than a salesperson who deflates each time he or she suffers a setback. The best performers bounce back from adversity, and even more important, they learn from it. Look for people who can tell you their story of resiliency. What setbacks have they experienced? How did they overcome that setback or obstacle? Can they explain clearly how they managed to bounce back and maintain a positive attitude?

Accountability — Holding others accountable is important, but being willing to hold oneself to the highest degree of accountability is a key trait of great salespeople. I look for people who will take ownership when they lose or when they make a mistake, and I don't like it when people blame everyone and everything but themselves for past failures. "What could I have done more effectively to achieve a better outcome?" is a question that great sellers ask themselves. Ask candidates about specific examples of self-accountability. Listen for excuse-makers and blame-assessors, and run as far away from them as possible.

Desire to be the best — Aside from the financial rewards, great salespeople generally derive satisfaction from being the best at what they do. They don't necessarily want to see others fail, but they do want to be at the top of the heap. They are driven to achieve things that others cannot. Ask candidates what really motivates them. If they say "money," then ask them what else motivates them. Money is certainly a motivator, but it is rarely the main motivator for real winners. Give them one more chance to tell you something like, "I want to beat / bury everyone else." If they cannot come up with an acceptable answer, they probably don't have the desire and drive required to be a long-term success.

Knowing how to create value — As my old colleagues at Huthwaite would say, "Diagnosis creates value." The best salespeople I know (and I know some of the best in the world) understand that they *really* earn their money in the earliest stages of the selling process when they help buyers to see things differently — to see problems they didn't know they had, opportunities about which they were previously unaware, solutions they could not have created on their own. Pay close attention to how they begin the interview. Have they prepared and thought about a way to frame our discussion that will lead us to a clear and positive outcome? What questions do they ask? Do they seek to understand what our definition of success is and what obstacles we have to overcome to get there? Do they offer creative or unique ideas about how to achieve our desired business outcomes? Do they seek to create value based on how they interview versus touting their many accomplishments? If so, you might have a value-creator on hand, and you should seriously consider him or her.

One of the best recruiters I've come to know is my friend Kim Cole, co-founder and one of the principals of The Sales Zone, a top sales recruiting firm in the mid-Atlantic region of the United States. Kim happened to recruit me to work for Huthwaite back in 2003. Kim and I worked on a series of advisory briefs for USR's customers recently, and she offered a simple six-step process for finding salespeople who will meet your needs for productive talent in our brief titled "Finding Sales Talent." Following is an excerpt:

Step One: Start with a great job description.
Before you start spending hours of your time searching for candidates on LinkedIn (or asking someone else in your company to do it for you), you need a well-written job description. Successful recruiting comes, in large part, through direct outreach. As a result, you need a great job description as a starting point for any employment discussion.

Your job description should showcase your company and the career opportunity that your firm has to offer. Think of a job description not only as a vehicle to communicate hiring needs and details about the role, but also as a marketing piece that will further expand your reputation as an employer of choice and represent your organization within the business community that you serve.

Step Two: Create a list of desired skills and recruiting resources.
The online world is keyword-driven. Give some thought to the types of words that describe the role you seek to fill. Work with your recruiting and human resources team to come up with a list of skills as well as desired companies from which you want to recruit.

Step Three: Craft a well-written pitch email/InMail.
Just as you would customize an email message to a prospective client, each and every communication to candidates must contain some form of customization if you really want an outreach campaign to be effective. Read their résumé or LinkedIn profile, pick out a skill or piece of experience that you like, and

incorporate it into the communication. Generic communication to prospective candidates rarely, if ever, works.

Step Four: Start searching and sourcing candidates.
Armed with your job description, you are ready to begin building a pipeline of prospective candidates with whom you'd like to start a conversation about the open sales role at your company. In addition to using LinkedIn's InMail feature, reach out to your personal and professional network using regular email.

Step Five: Focus on follow-up .
When someone responds to an inquiry, a twenty-four-hour response time is important. Even if it is simply to request a résumé or to acknowledge that you'll be in touch soon, saying thank you to the candidate's follow-up is crucial. Remember, your company's brand and your personal brand are at stake with every candidate interaction.

Step Six: Start interviewing.
You probably have at least a few worthy candidates you can start interviewing. Congratulations! Your hard work has paid off.

Kim offered this last bit of advice on the process for recruiting top talent: "In order to maximize your investment of time and energy, you will want to ensure that you have an interview process in place that moves candidates from interviewing to hiring at a professional cadence. Remember, your company's brand is on the line with each candidate interaction. What's more, candidates can now evaluate your company's interview process on Glassdoor and other social media outlets, so you want to interview them as though your entire company were under the lens of evaluation with each person passing through the door. Here are three quick tips to ensure a tight hiring process: 1) Tell candidates *upfront* what the entire interview process looks like — from the people who will evaluate them to pre- and post-offer paperwork. 2) Engage only key stakeholders in the interviewing process. If you have more than three to five people interviewing and evaluating candidates, try to streamline things. 3) Say thank you! Whether you decide to hire someone or not, he or she has taken time to interview with your company. Don't allow candidates to exit your process without properly acknowledging their investment of time."

Once you've selected your team members, the next step to building a powerful team is being able to clearly explain the fundamental ways in which the team and organization operate. This can be a good way to set expectations as early as possible in the recruiting process to gauge fit. Once you've selected your team members, the next step to building a powerful team is being able to clearly explain the fundamental ways in which the team and organization operate. This can be a good way to set expectations as early as possible in the recruiting process to gauge fit. You should be able to explain the sales process, coaching cycle, and your sales organization's expectations for sales behavior. If you've done your homework and mastered the concepts outlined previously in this book, you should be able to do this easily. And just the act of having and communicating this type of information in a conscious way will set the stage for people who respond to this type of environment to rise up from the recruitment pool.

Monitoring whether hires can stick to the program and operating rhythm and fit into the culture is another early indicator of whether they will likely become positive contributors over time. Inability to catch up with and stick with the sales organization's operating rhythm or to conform to the company's culture of planning and value creation might be an early warning signal. I am not saying that you have to rid yourself of people who are slow to catch up to the team's rhythm, but I would recommend that you consider the old axiom "Hire slowly and fire quickly." The time you will cost yourself trying to rescue someone who cannot — or will not — help themselves is extremely valuable, and your investment might not pay off.

CHAPTER 7

Building a Coaching Culture

An Outwardly Focused Task

Carl Singer is the head of sales and marketing for Maplehurst Bakeries, a large business unit within the Weston Foods family of companies. I have been a coach and advisor to Carl and his sales leadership team for six years. Carl rose through the ranks of the organization over the course of two decades, eventually taking the sales leadership helm after some acquisitions and consolidation of sales teams. The newly consolidated sales team had three previous leaders, each with a somewhat different approach. The company's growth goals were aggressive by the standards of the food industry, and Carl and his team knew that in order to grow sales rapidly, they would need a common process for selling and the most effective salesforce in their industry.

The company made an investment, like many others do, in sales training that taught the sales team to plan more effectively, to ask better questions, to listen, and to develop needs. Like many other sales training efforts, the impact of the training was difficult to measure. The perception after the first round of the training initiative was that the process was perhaps too complex, and salespeople were not adopting the new approach as the sales leadership team had hoped. Carl and his team, including Dennis Currens and Lance Strefling, knew that they had to find a way to break the complex system down into something more digestible. "We needed a more practical and pragmatic approach" to developing the skills of the salesforce, according to Carl.

Carl and his sales leadership team concluded that they needed perhaps less "training" and more coaching. A coach would be better able to help a salesperson adapt and apply the company's sales process in the context of real-world scenarios and sales opportunities. Sales managers, much like their salespeople, did not develop their skills or follow through in a consistent way, so the Maplehurst sales leadership team made a commitment to build a coaching culture and continually improve the sales coaching function within the organization. It would become one of its great competitive differentiators.

"We had to commit to excellence in coaching to ensure our ability to develop salespeople, especially new hires," Carl said. "We needed to do so not just for consistency's sake but also for purposes of growth and succession." Carl and his team were developing an excellent sales team not just for today but for the foreseeable future.

The sales leadership team has seen some changes in personnel over the last six years, but the group has consistently increased in its effectiveness. As the business has evolved, Carl and his sales leadership team have been able to continually develop and adjust where and how they are developing their salespeople. The coaching culture began to take hold shortly after Carl and his team made their commitment to excellence, and it stands strong today. The Maplehurst salesforce has delivered five consecutive years of record sales growth and leads all of its peer businesses in sales growth over the same period. Carl and his eleven-person sales leadership team all attribute the organization's great success to the commitment they have made to coaching and to their ability to refine their processes, behaviors, norms, and therefore, their culture. Salespeople value the coaching and support that they receive from their sales managers, and the organization is well-positioned for continued growth largely because of its coaching culture.

As in sports, music, dance, and most other disciplines that require ongoing commitment and hard work, coaching is a key enabler to great performance in professional sales.

Over the last several years, the professional selling community has been catching up to this notion. In a 2016 Sales Management Association study, respondents ranked sales coaching as the most important competency for sales managers. Survey respondents rated the importance of sales coaching versus other competency training (e.g., assessing seller performance, pipeline management, and leadership), and they gave sales coaching a rating of 5.8 on a scale of 7 points.

Even with the increased focus and spending on sales coaching competency development, moving the needle on coaching effectiveness is not easy. In fact, as organizations invest in sales coaching development, a common conclusion that sales and training leaders draw over time is that not everyone can or should be a coach. Coaching requires patience, self-awareness, humility, and a desire for improvement that exceeds one's desire to maintain the status quo. Coaching can be intimidating, even scary, for some because it requires a degree of openness to change and personal growth with which many of us are not totally comfortable.

For as much risk and exposure that sales coaching can create for a sales manager, a similar measure of exposure exists for those being coached. A productive coaching relationship requires that there be a "safe zone" between the coach and the performer, a certain level of mutual trust that enables the sort of candid feedback and commitment to action required for positive, intentional change in performance. Considering the competing demands in a sales organization that I described earlier, life on a sales floor or in the field hardly feels safe. The sales manager has to create an environment that allows mistakes to occur without impacting customers. It is a very delicate balance.

Coaching in professional sales comes with certain challenges, some of which are universal and cross-disciplinary and some of which are very specific to the task of coaching salespeople.

One of the greatest temptations for professional sales coaches is to step in and take over, to demonstrate what great looks like while the salesperson observes. However, this violates the "safe zone" principle because it demonstrates to the salesperson that the coach has no faith or trust in her ability to do the job. It also leads the salesperson to determine there is no value in the coaching she received because the coach just took everything away from her and did it himself. Doing the selling for the salesperson doesn't actually show or teach the salesperson anything. Sales is learned by doing, not watching.

A rule of thumb to help you be effective as a coach: If you have arranged to participate in a sales call as a coach, sit back, be quiet, observe, and share your feedback privately with the salesperson after the call. Do anything else and you are selling, not coaching.

One of the more challenging commitments a sales coach must make is to maintain a consistent rhythm with those you are coaching. This might sound like a simple task, but it can be deceptively challenging. Once you factor in the normal distractions, customer-related issues, and other responsibilities facing a sales manager on a day-to-day basis, you will begin to understand why it can be so difficult to maintain the following, simple rhythm:

Plan with the salesperson. Whether you are planning an upcoming call, planning a competitive strategy to win a piece of new business, or planning a key account strategy, supporting a salesperson by simply being there while he or she is planning can reap huge rewards.

Observe. When the situation is right, observing a salesperson as he or she executes the call you've planned or the strategy you've hatched together can provide extremely valuable insight into how to improve performance. Is it possible to coach without observing people in action? Certainly. However, the feedback a coach is able to offer after observing someone in action will be more specific, more targeted to the real needs of the person being coached and generally more valuable to the salesperson (assuming feedback is delivered in an effective way; we'll get to that later).

Review the outcome. What better way is there to measure the effectiveness of a plan and its execution than to look at its outcome? This is what the most effective sales managers do. They ask questions like the ones below to ensure ongoing focus on achieving important outcomes with customers and to create helpful insights for the salesperson.

- Did we achieve the outcome we wanted?

- Why or why not?

- What is the next outcome we seek to achieve?

- How can we ensure that we are able to achieve that outcome?

Reinforce skills and role-play. Have you ever played a round of golf without first visiting the driving range or the practice green? Have you ever participated in a recital without warming up or walking through your music or your steps? In a similar way, professional selling without regular practice, reinforcement, and live walk-throughs or role-playing leaves a seller unprepared to perform at his or her best. Part of the role of a coach is to ensure that sellers have opportunities to practice and reinforce their skills, preferably in the context of the real-world opportunities that they address on the job. But how many sales managers actually create an environment where role-playing, practice, and reinforcement are a normal and required element of doing the job of professional selling? In our experience, the answer is "not nearly enough." Skill reinforcement and role-playing are often sidelined by events, overtaken by the day-to-day tasks and reactivity that is often a part of selling.

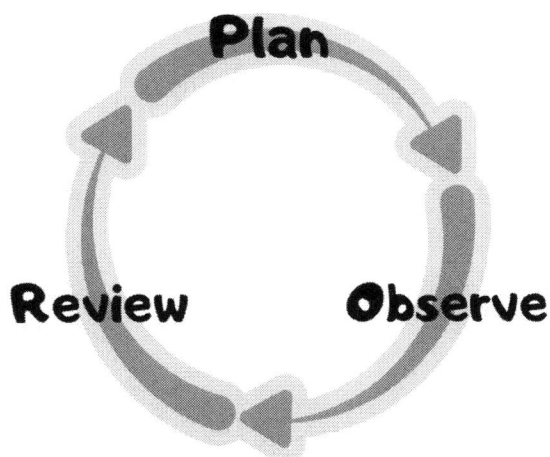

Building and maintaining a coaching culture are long-term tasks where the benefits increase over time. Coaching, like complex sales, is akin to a golf swing. One cannot master all aspects of a golf swing all at once, and any attempt to do so will tend to result in disaster (think massive slices or hooks, topped golf balls, and generally ugly scores). The same is true in coaching salespeople.

Coaching mastery requires patience and focus. A sales management team must identify specific themes, norms, and behaviors that they will commit to together in order to establish a coaching culture. A coaching culture tends to start taking hold when sales leadership identifies that one key change that will deliver a positive and immediate result. It is unrealistic to expect a team of sales managers to make wholesale change in the way they approach their roles, so establishing a coaching culture is required. A tangible example of this comes from one of my longtime clients, a manufacturer in the food business. This particular organization is in a highly competitive and commoditized space, and its only true competitive differentiator is its sales organization. In order to ensure that the sales team is continually improving, the sales leadership team — from frontline sales managers up to the head of sales — is also continually improving.

From the top down, all members of the sales management team set the expectation that their respective teams will be coached. In return, their sales teams expect that coaching to be of high value, and the sales management teams and salespeople push each other to plan, think critically, ask good questions, and listen to each other. The result is a sales organization that is clear about where it has opportunities to improve, a plan for achieving that improvement, and perhaps most important, a sales organization that far exceeds the professionalism, preparedness, and execution of its competitors.

Put simply, this organization's coaching culture is the driver for its success in the market, and all sales managers in the organization will point to the expectations, norms, and behaviors that they have committed to as sales leaders as the root cause for their success.

In companies where salespeople expect to be coached and receive effective coaching, the results speak for themselves. Sales organizations I have cited in this book such as Maplehurst Bakeries, Platts, and IBM Software Group all achieved outsize growth compared to their competitors based in no small part on their ability to establish coaching cultures. Their salespeople win deals that they otherwise would not have won, and internal relationships are strong and collaborative.

Establishing a coaching rhythm in which sales managers and salespeople stay in a steady loop of planning, execution, review, and more planning is the simplest way to build and sustain a coaching culture. And you can start building that culture and that rhythm today, by doing the following:

1. Commit to the idea of practice and reinforcement, and do so within the context of real-world scenarios. Consider the role coaching can play while

your team is practicing.

2. Look at your calendar right now and identify the periods where you can carve out time for this practice and coaching. Make sure it is a sustainable and repeatable time slot on your calendar; otherwise, it will be overcome by events and get lost in future schedules.

3. Before you provide coaching or feedback to a member of your team, take a second to put yourself in his or her shoes. Imagine you've just finished a sales call (real or role-played), and you know your coach was observing and taking notes. You're understandably a little nervous about what your coach will say, but you are open to feedback that will make you a better salesperson. Does your coach put you at ease?

Any advice on improvements or adjustments will be best received by the salesperson if you start with positive feedback, build his or her confidence, and establish or solidify trust. Follow this by asking questions about how the salesperson felt about the call and whether she can identify any areas where she was unsure or realizes in retrospect that she missed an opportunity. Using this "pull" style of communication allows the coach to guide salespeople toward conclusions she wants them to reach. The effect is greater commitment to fixing the issues on the part of the salesperson, as well as a positive association with the process of coaching.

A sustainable coaching culture can be characterized by the positive nature of the relationship between the coach and salespeople. Descriptors such as collaborative, healthy, value creating, open, candid, and positive are typical labels we apply to winning coaching cultures. Conversely, command and control cultures where coaching is not part of the organizational DNA can be described in roughly opposite terms such as combative, unhealthy, commoditizing, political, risky, and draining. Which type of culture would you choose to work for? Which type do you want to build within your own sales organization?

CHAPTER 8

Leading by Example

An Outwardly Focused Task

arry Letow is the CEO of Convergence Technology and the chief sales officer of its sister business, Intelligent ID. Convergence is a nationally recognized provider of IT virtualization and cybersecurity, and it is one of the top commercial and federal integrators in the country.

Larry began his career as a salesperson, and he leads his salespeople with authenticity. "I don't ask people to do anything I am not willing to do or haven't already done myself. As I hire new salespeople into our organization, I have to be authentic when I describe this job — what's great about it and what's hard about it."

"As sales leaders, we have to serve as an example for our salespeople to model their behaviors after, or they will likely not succeed." Larry describes the need for sales leaders, whether they are frontline managers or the head of sales, to help salespeople adapt the sales process to their personal style. Some of his people lean toward the social, entertaining end of the personality spectrum while others are deeply technical, serious players who interact differently with clients.

When the time came to introduce a new security product to the market, the challenge was very clear. "We had to think and sell differently because we were becoming a product sales organization after being a services sales organization for so many years. We had to move to a recurring software license sale, which was a big leap for some of my team."

The Convergence/Intelligent ID team also had to adapt to a new buyer and a new buying conversation. Where the group had comfort in the past speaking with mid-level IT department buyers, it now had to engage with a more senior line of business executives. This was an entirely different kind of conversation, and many of the existing salespeople lacked the necessary confidence to engage with senior-level clients about strategic business issues.

"I made sure I was involved in planning and supporting the closing of the first sale in every new segment we called upon," Larry said. "I knew I had to be the first salesperson out of the gate, selling our new product. If I can't sell it, how can I motivate or coach others to sell it?"

When Larry demonstrated what it took to sell the new security product, it had an impact on the confidence and performance of the team that even he did not fully expect.

"The sales team believed our new product could be successfully sold because I showed them it could be done." Larry does not claim to have gone about every sales opportunity perfectly, but he pursued each one with the kind of focus, intensity, conviction, and enthusiasm that he expected his salespeople to demonstrate. The net effect was that the members of his sales team opened their minds to how they could execute this entirely new and different kind of sale, and they had the confidence and a model to follow to do it themselves. The Convergence/Intelligent ID sales team continues to receive positive recognition from partners and clients to this day as a result of Larry's leadership by example.

"Leading by example means I understand what the salespeople are going through," he said. "By being in the trenches with them, I can be a better leader, and I also gain a great deal more personal satisfaction and excitement. I know that I have made an impact when the team follows my lead."

If a sales manager wants his or her salespeople to be thoughtful, to think strategically, to plan, and to execute with excellence, then he or she must also model that same behavior. Because, once again, when sales managers demonstrate bad behavior — regardless of their words — they will get bad behavior from their teams.

Consider a few real-world examples that illustrate the difference between walking the talk and not. Greg Lanz is the vice president of global sales and marketing for Modular Mining, a software and technology company that sells to the mining industry. I have worked with Greg for the last five years, coaching and supporting sales and business development staff in North America and other regions such as Australia and South Africa. Greg has been the chief champion for the customer-centric, value-oriented approach to selling based on Neil Rackham's research for many years. An engineering-dominant culture pervades Modular, and that has, at times, made the journey from a deeply technical and product-focused sales organization to a solution-oriented one very challenging. But Greg has never wavered in his commitment to planning, coaching, and accountability. A lesser sales leader would not have been able to lead the sales organization through such a period, in which the company has survived down markets and heavy, price-driven competition.

Contrast Greg's example with a different head of sales whom I came to know several years ago from another tech-heavy, engineering-focused firm in Pennsylvania. (I have to leave out names to protect the guilty in this example.) This particular sales leader spoke eloquently and forcefully about the need for the sales organization to focus on the customer and to create value based on how they sell versus what they sell. He charged his sales training manager to develop an intricate and detailed implementation plan replete with reinforcement activities and coaching forums for sales managers. The "Future Value" initiative was launched. No sooner had he delivered his message about value creation and the need for change than he went right back to his own ineffective habits. He rarely planned. He never coached, and he pushed his salespeople to discount the firm's services whenever there was pressure from a customer to do so. The firm's sales staff quickly concluded that this initiative had no legs whatsoever. They simply ducked, waited for all the talk and hype about value creation and customer focus to pass, and went right back to the same old ineffective habits that put them at a competitive disadvantage. Two years later, that sales leader was terminated, the business was restructured, and unfortunately, a large number of staff members were also let go.

I consider people like Greg Lanz, Larry Letow, Jeff Lautenbach, and Carl Singer to be transformational leaders. Transformational leaders think "how" first, before they think "what." In other words, they know that their success hinges not necessarily on *what* methodology or performance framework they choose, but on *how* they execute that methodology or framework. They are highly disciplined in the way they communicate, lead, and follow through on change. Hence, they are able to transform their sales organizations in a way that others simply cannot. They are authentic in their approaches to others because they are comfortable in their own skin, and they maintain the highest level of integrity in their dealings with customers, staff, and partners.

How many of us who lead sales teams today can say that we are totally authentic and maintain our integrity all the time? How many take shortcuts when the right way might be just a few small additional steps? How many miss out on the huge rewards that discipline and commitment render time after time?

CHAPTER 9

Establishing the
Discipline of Planning

An Outwardly Focused Task

From his days as an investment consultant at his family-owned firm, Brendan Clark knew how to tap into the motivations of financial advisors. He knew intuitively that in order to differentiate himself and his firm's offerings from the competition, he had to be able to connect what was personally important to each advisor and each of that advisor's clients with what Clark Capital Management had to offer. Over a period of two decades, Brendan rose through the ranks of the firm, eventually becoming an executive vice president, then president, and ultimately CEO. When the firm's sales and revenues were down below expectations a few years ago, Brendan was tasked with addressing the problem. The firm had to significantly increase assets under management, and it had to do so in the face of headwinds that affected the market as a whole and some of Clark's products in particular.

The firm's past successes had actually masked some performance problems in the sales organization. Investment consultants were overly reliant on features and the performance of the firm's products. Faced with an uphill battle to increase sales, the team's morale was lower than Brendan could accept. "Our psychology was not where it needed to be. We weren't very confident." Reflecting on what needed to change, Brendan said, "The team needed to change its habits."

He identified one very specific and important area in which behavior needed to change, and it was in the area of planning. The team was (or had become) somewhat undisciplined when it came to planning. Call planning or opportunity planning were done haphazardly, and there was little evidence to suggest that much planning was being done except for those circumstances when Brendan forced the issue by proposing and participating in sales planning sessions.

"We needed advisors to buy from us because of the value we could deliver to them and their clients." So Brendan needed the team to commit to planning, a process he named the "Value Creation Process." The objective of the new planning discipline was simply to get his wholesalers to think differently about their consultative approach to selling. They would start by concentrating time and energy on seeking to discover a few important things about every advisor they called upon. "Simply knowing the other person's motivation was something we had to do better."

"Salespeople need to be innately curious," he said. "Some of my people struggle with that because it is not their natural orientation to selling." This planning process would be very different from the somewhat less disciplined approach investment consultants had taken in the past. "We had to look at sales through a completely different lens."

"Reluctance to change was huge," he added. Certain individuals went as far as to say that their style of selling (e.g., not focusing on the other party's motivation) would come back into vogue when the market turned in a more positive direction. And so, Brendan's Value Creation Process and initiative faced headwinds of its own.

His approach was to gain small commitments to planning over the course of a roughly six- to nine-month period, rather than to install changes in a wholesale manner. For example, at first he only required a Value Creation plan for specific, strategically important meetings with advisors. In this way Brendan was able to lay the groundwork for the firm's future growth. Slowly but surely, they would become a more disciplined and effective sales organization by virtue of making a series of small, digestible commitments to planning and acting upon those plans.
Planning can have an immediate impact on performance, but we have to be realistic in the degree to which we expect salespeople to become great planners and critical thinkers. One of the key lessons we can learn from Brendan's experience is that committing to the discipline of planning requires a patient and deliberate approach, or the commitment to planning might waver.

In my experience, the best, most disciplined sales leadership teams commit collectively to **what they will do** and **what they will not do**. Their activities and focus are consistent in good times and in bad times. They do not waver from the practices and behaviors that correlate to great outcomes, and they regularly work past obstacles to maintaining discipline because they know how important being disciplined is for those who want to succeed.

The notion that discipline leads to success is no great revelation. Like so many other things in life and in business, however, talking about being disciplined and actually being disciplined are two different things. In order to establish and maintain discipline as a sales leader, one must define the various levels at which planning

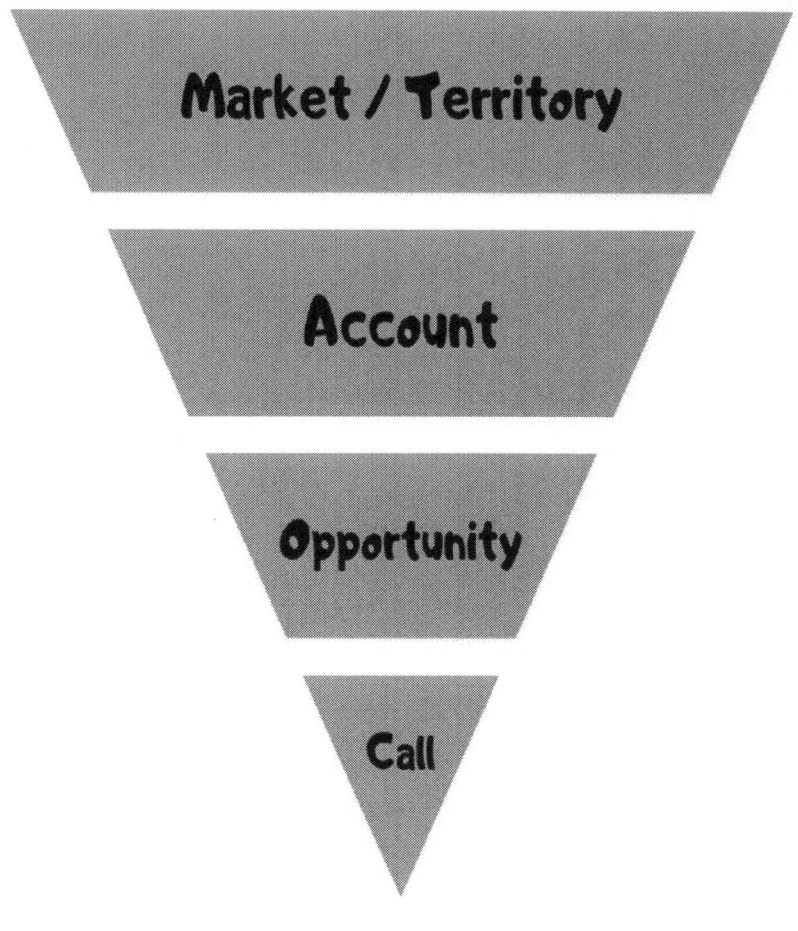

must occur and address what can get in the way at each level of planning.

There are several levels of planning in which a sales manager can participate and deliver high value to his or her sales organization:

- **Market/Territory Planning**

Planning at the market or territory level entails identifying all of the potential opportunities or opportunity types that salespeople should be expected to pursue. This level of planning typically takes place annually or on some lengthy interval during which market or territory assignments are doled out to salespeople. It is also typically performed at the same time that goals, including financial objectives and quotas, are being assigned to salespeople.

In very effective organizations, market or territory-level planning takes into account the company's GTM, available resources, and capacity to serve customers, as well as its stretch financial objectives when planning how to cover a market and carve out appropriate territories.

- **Account Planning**

Account planning in many organizations tends to be an annual or otherwise infrequent, periodic process by which management extracts somewhat useful information from the salesforce about key customer relationships. Once that information is extracted, sales management plays little to no role in helping that account plan succeed. Salespeople derive some value but not very much from the process.

In the most effective sales organizations, account planning is a more frequent and more valuable process by which sales teams develop and launch effective strategies for growth, based on their ability to address issues and opportunities that are strategically important to their customers. Managers play the role of facilitator and thought partner, and they establish and maintain focus on more than just the first or immediate sale but on the overall growth of the customer relationship.

A manager can be instrumental in the successful growth of a customer relationship simply by ensuring that the right resources (people) are in place to achieve that growth. Helping to assemble an account team that has what it takes to develop a long-term relationship with a customer might be one of the most important things a manager can do.

A sales manager can create great value for salespeople simply by helping them connect the dots between certain strategically important customer problems and the capabilities that they can bring to bear for the customer. In a sense, they can help salespeople step far enough back from the trees to see the forest in front of them. They can help salespeople see the "big picture" and plot a strategy that will help their customer achieve big success.

Ensuring that the right resources are in place to ensure account growth is an ongoing task rather than a one-time event, and the most effective managers today are in the habit of evaluating account team assignments on a regular basis. From there, setting account growth goals, regularly reviewing account teams' progress toward those goals, holding teams accountable to their plans, and creating insight for those teams along the way are vital elements of the sales leader's job.

• Opportunity Planning

Opportunity planning is about winning the deal, and it is somewhat limited in scope compared to account-level planning. Sales managers can be instrumental in helping sales teams win opportunities they might not otherwise win.

Opportunity planning is also an ideal forum in which to create value for salespeople. In the context of winning the deal, a sales manager can help a salesperson discover unrecognized problems in his or her approach, see opportunities to expand the size of the deal or increase the value of the solution, and arrive at new or creative ways to achieve the desired outcome. Sales managers are also uniquely suited by virtue of their role to broker necessary and valuable resources that salespeople might not otherwise be able to access.

The fine balance, of course, in opportunity planning is for sales managers to coach and not to do the thinking for the salesperson. A classic mistake that I see sales managers make every day is prescribing next steps for salespeople to win their opportunities when they should be leading salespeople to conclusions about what they need to do to win. After all, whose opportunity is it?

• Call Planning

While this is the most tactical form of planning in which a sales manager can engage with salespeople, call planning is also a tremendous opportunity to create value for salespeople.

This also happens to be the ideal place for modeling the right behavior. If we expect our salespeople to plan smart questions that lead to important conclusions and commitments that move the deal forward, then we must model the same behavior. Remember our model for influencing behavior from Chapter 2 in this book? It features Conclusions, Questions, and Actions, and regardless of which sales methodology your organization adheres to (e.g., SPIN, Solution Selling, or your own in-house methodology), this simple framework applies as well to call planning as it does to coaching in general.

As you consider the different levels of planning and the coaching opportunities that each level presents, consider if you are approaching those opportunities to coach as effectively and consistently as you should be. If there is opportunity to improve, you'll have some time and space to think about exactly how you can improve when you reach the *Sales Leadership Excellence Planner* at the end of this book.

CHAPTER 10

Motivating Others and Keeping Them Motivated

An Outwardly Focused Task

The task of motivating salespeople comes in two forms: motivating individuals and motivating the whole team or organization, depending on the scope of one's leadership responsibility. The task of motivating the individual is primarily what I will focus on in this chapter. One of the worst mistakes that I've seen sales leaders make is to assume that their salespeople are internally motivated and willing to work hard enough to achieve excellence. The reality is there are some members of virtually every sales team who are externally motivated, meaning they need an external force (e.g., a cheerleader, a reward, or a consequence) to help with their personal motivation. For those salespeople who are more externally motivated than they are self-motivated, the sales manager must help the individual salesperson recognize the personal value or WIIFM ("What's In It For Me") of Excellence.

If one has attempted to pursue excellence in any pursuit or discipline (e.g., sports, music, academics, relationships), one knows that there is a big difference between wanting to be excellent and doing what it takes to actually be excellent. Some call this the *Knowing-Doing Gap*, and it is a huge barrier for sales leaders who want to have highly motivated teams. Very simply, the WIIFM of Excellence can be defined as:

the need for every salesperson to understand the personal payoff, advantage, or benefit that they will receive in return for working harder at their craft. Call it their WIIFM or their clear vision of personal success.

Think of the framework for influencing others from Chapter 2 again, and we're going to apply it directly to the task of motivating a salesperson.

- **What conclusion(s) do I want this salesperson to draw?**

  For example, I want this salesperson to recognize that there is great personal payoff associated with being more disciplined and planning each and every call he makes on customers, despite the fact that he thinks it takes too long.

- **What questions will I ask him or her to lead to that conclusion?**

  I will ask: Can you tell me about the outcome of the important meeting we had last week (that I know you didn't plan for and that ended badly)? Why did it end badly? Can you tell me what you did to plan for that meeting? Would it have been possible to anticipate the customer's pushback and change the outcome of the meeting? How much time did you invest in traveling to meet the customer, putting together a slide deck, and preparing your talk-track? How much time did it take you to earn that meeting in the first place?

- **What actions do I want him or her to take?**

  What can you do differently in a similar situation next time? How would planning or approaching your plan differently help you? How else would it help you, etc.? What will you differently next time, and how can I be helpful along the way?

From this example, you might infer that motivating salespeople has little to do with giving a Knute Rockne-like speech or demanding excellence from them, and you would be partially correct. While there are certainly times to rouse an individual or a whole team of salespeople with a motivating talk, those scenarios come far less often than the day-to-day opportunities to tap into a seller's personal motivation. It is a far more powerful form of motivation when a salesperson concludes, "I can do more, and I *will* do more because it benefits me personally." Much of the task of motivating others comes down to helping them see the personal value of going the extra mile — or even just the extra foot — to achieve something better.

What about when you need to give the big motivational talk? Let's face it: Some of us are better at the big motivating talk than others. For as much training as I've received and practice I've applied to the big talk, I know that I am just pretty good at giving the motivational speech. Mike, my first sales manager coming out of college, was the kind of guy who could motivate people to run through walls to meet the team's objectives. He was big, loud, and a little bit crude at times, but every member of his team, myself included, got a big motivational kick when he got the team together to give the big talk. Do yourself a favor and watch the famous scene in "Boiler Room" when Vin Diesel visits the sales floor to give the team a motivational boost. He bears a remarkable resemblance to my first sales manager.

But that is just not who I am. I can speak with excitement, intensity, enthusiasm, sincerity, and conviction, but I am not particularly boisterous or demonstrative in my speaking style, particularly in front of groups. My style is more conversational, so for me, the big team talk has to look quite a bit different from the big team speeches that my old boss Mike used to give. I know that I need to tap into the team's sense of responsibility and to get them to consent to a clear vision of success that includes each and every one of them playing a key role in our collective win.

This vision includes not only the clear business and financial outcomes we want to achieve (e.g., deliver $X of revenue by end of the calendar year or exceed our financial objective of $Y million) but also what we want to achieve in terms of our relationships with customers, our share in the competitive marketplace, and so forth. The WIIFM for every member of the sales team has to include a clear answer to the question, "What is in it for me personally if we succeed together?" More than simply their personal WIIFM, each member of the team needs to feel, *down to the core of his being,* what it will feel like to be a member of a winning team.

Some members of your sales team understand this intuitively. Others will need you to help them understand what is in it for them to stretch for excellence and to be great teammates along the way. Following is a simple recipe for motivating the entire team, even if you cannot rely on your ability to give the big team talk:

- Make sure that you, as the sales manager, have a crystal-clear vision of success, clear objectives, and clearly defined roles and responsibilities for management and sales staff. This will create an environment where the entire team will operate at peak levels. And success is its own motivational force, so it provides a self-perpetuating system.

- Capturing and celebrating successes motivate salespeople to make time for the right behavior. In this way, you can make a clear connection between the right behavior and the desired outcome. Simply celebrating a closed sale on the basis that it closed is not necessarily a winning strategy because you could end up celebrating sales that came about in the wrong way. For example, if a salesperson steeply discounted in order to win despite the team's objective to preserve margin in every opportunity, that would not be a scenario in which the sales manager would want to celebrate success. This would serve to erode the commitment from the team. When you define success as **having positive**

outcomes based on the right behaviors and celebrate those differently from sales based on the "wrong" behavior, that becomes a culture that reinforces itself and is motivating.

- Establishing a system of rewards and consequences results in good outcomes. There will be great examples to celebrate, and there will be not-so-great examples of behavior you want to squelch. Communicate with your team about your system of rewards and consequences. If we are going to celebrate and reward the right behavior, what kinds of rewards are going to be relevant for the team? For individuals? If members of the team violate our code of behavior, what consequences will they be bringing upon themselves? It might not sound like a fun conversation, but it is one that needs to be had if a team is going to have a clear system of rewards and consequences. Every successful team that I have ever observed or been part of had some system of rewards and consequences, and team members were committed to following through on it together.

- Being vulnerable and admitting that perfection isn't attainable. My friend and longtime colleague Daniel Grissom is a renowned speaker and world-class sales trainer. I've heard him tell audiences he trains, "Perfection is not required, but excellence will be accepted." This is a great summary of what I've seen great coaches reflect to their sales teams. By willingly and intentionally sharing your own stories — especially stories of mistakes you've made and lessons learned that were later leveraged into wins — you can provide a powerful, personal witness of what it takes to be successful.

CHAPTER 11

Fine-Tuning Your Operating Rhythm

Final Thoughts

Remember Jeff Lautenbach from the first chapter? Ever since that day roughly ten years ago when Jeff concluded that changing his organization's cadence could enable him to focus on the most important things first, he has gone on to lead large global sales teams, applying the same principle but in somewhat different ways that were appropriate to the situation and his organization's desired business outcome.

Jeff describes the conclusion he came to back in his days as a vice president for a large region at IBM Software Group: "It was really transformational for me." Jeff's career trajectory post-IBM tells a story of a leader who continually takes on the task of creating world-class sales organizations. From leading the enterprise sales organization at Salesforce, to the head of the CRM business at SAP, chief revenue officer at HC1, to president of worldwide field operations at Jive Software, Jeff has learned that there is no one universal cadence that applies to all companies and all scenarios.

Based on Jeff's experiences and my own observations over the course of the last seven years, we share similar views on what shapes the cadence (or impacts the operating rhythm) of a sales organization. Simply, we can express these in the following questions:

- What are we trying to achieve? What is our vision of success?

- What value are we trying to create for our customers?
- Is there a way we can expand value by exposing certain problems or opportunities for our prospects and customers?
- If these are the right areas of focus for our internal collaboration and coaching activities, then how can we ensure our cadence allows enough time to focus on them?

In one of the more recent examples in Jeff's story, the business needed to focus on the process by which sales development reps (SDRs) handed off valuable intelligence gained from prospect conversations. In those conversations, prospects shared important information about problems they were trying to solve. And so Jeff's organizational cadence needed to include time to focus on collaboration and planning between SDRs and the account executives who would carry the next dialogue with the prospective customer. "In these conversations, SDRs and account executives discussed where the customer was in their buying journey. How does the customer get from their 'as-is' to their 'to-be' state?"

These crucial conversations could not be left to chance, so Jeff made sure that his entire team's cadence was built around the vitally important, internal collaboration that focused the team's thinking around customer problems and opportunities.

Once a sales manager establishes a consistent operating rhythm with her or his team, he or she must actively diagnose ways in which the team's time, focus, approaches, and communication might need to adapt according to the ways in which its environment changes over time.

My Sales Leadership Excellence Plan

In each chapter of this book, I have shared a story to illustrate one of the fundamental ways in which great sales managers separate themselves from average managers. I also offered my specific thoughts and some guidance on how to incorporate these fundamentals into your operating rhythm with your team.

Without knowing the specifics of your particular situation, your team dynamics, and so forth, perhaps the best way in which I can help you come to specific conclusions about how you can improve as a leader of salespeople is to offer some questions for your consideration.

I will break these questions down into three basic categories:

- What should I keep doing (because it is working well)?

- What should I stop doing (because it is getting in the way of excellence)?
- What should I start doing or change (because there is room for improvement)?

If we consider those three questions for each of the fundamental areas of sales leadership excellence, we have a process for developing a concrete action plan for your specific team and situation. Starting on the next page you'll find your Sales Leadership Excellence Planner. On each page of the planner, you will find the questions and some space where you can jot down the specific activites, ideas, or actions that you will keep doing, stop doing, or change.

I hope that this book and the *Sales Leadership Excellence Planner* will help you arrive at some clarity about the ways in which you can be a more effective sales leader immediately. You might have identified some changes that are quick and easy, and I recommend you make those changes immediately after setting this book down. There might be other changes you've identified that will take more time or will be really challenging for you to execute.

My advice to you is: Don't be afraid. Just get started. Change takes time, and the only way you will fail at becoming a better leader is if you take no action at all. If certain changes you've identified will take time or be difficult, give yourself some specific and time-based goals and make incremental changes. Your team and your results will benefit from each and every positive change that you make. The choice to be excellent, of course, is all yours.

Sales Leadership Excellence Planner

Finding My Operating Rhythm

What activities with my team are leading directly to positive results (e.g., team collaboration, opportunity planning, weekly deal reviews)?

Things I will keep doing...

Sales Leadership Excellence Planner

Finding My Operating Rhythm

> What activities with my team are having a negative impact on results or wasting otherwise productive time?
>
> Things I will stop doing...

Sales Leadership Excellence Planner

CHAPTER 1
Finding My Operating Rhythm

How can I improve our team's interactions to make them more productive and directly lead to positive outcomes?

How can I ensure that important activities get priority treatment, taking precedence over low-value or time-wasting activities?

Things I will start doing or change...

CHAPTER 2
Leading with Influence

What types of communication are having the most positive effect on my team's behavior? What am I doing to help my team members draw new or different conclusions about their roles and their behavior?

Things I will keep doing...

CHAPTER 2
Leading with Influence

What examples of "push" or other ineffective methods of influencing others am I using frequently on the job? What is getting in the way of my ability to influence the behavior of my team?

Things I will stop doing...

CHAPTER 2
Leading with Influence

How can I improve my ability to influence the team's behavior? How can I plan and execute more effectively when I need to influence the team's thinking or behavior?

Things I will start doing or change...

CHAPTER 3
Using Data and Metrics to Guide My Sales Team

What information/data/metrics am I using that help me diagnose team or individual performance issues efficiently and accurately?

Things I will keep doing...

CHAPTER 3
Using Data and Metrics to Guide My Sales Team

What data/metrics are not particularly helpful for diagnosing performance? What data/metrics are not directly connected with the results I expect my team to deliver?

Things I will stop doing...

CHAPTER 3
Using Data and Metrics to Guide My Sales Team

How can I make better use of information/data/metrics to diagnose team performance issues?

How can I better use data/metrics to identify new opportunities or new ways to achieve the results we want?

Things I will start doing or change...

CHAPTER 4
Aligning My Sales Team with Our Go-to-Market

What can we do to continue our emphasis on pursuing the right types of opportunities for our business?

Things I will keep doing...

CHAPTER 4
Aligning My Sales Team with Our Go-to-Market

What types of opportunities should we stop pursuing? How can I help the team stop the practice of pursuing opportunities that are wrong for us?

Things I will stop doing...

CHAPTER 4
Aligning My Sales Team with Our Go-to-Market

What can I do to encourage my team members to focus on the right opportunities?

What conclusions do I need them to draw about the cost of pursuing the wrong opportunities?

What questions will I ask them?

What support will I provide them as they pursue the right opportunities?

Things I will start doing or change...

CHAPTER 5
Creating Maximum Value for My Team

What am I doing to build trust with the members of my team?

What am I doing to help them see problems or opportunities they otherwise would not recognize?

What new or different approaches to their challenges am I helping them come up with?

What resources am I good at finding or brokering for the team?

Things I will keep doing...

CHAPTER 5
Creating Maximum Value for My Team

What am I doing to erode trust with members of my team? In what ways are my interactions with my team not valuable?

Things I will stop doing...

CHAPTER 5
Creating Maximum Value for My Team

How can I more effectively help my team members see unrecognized problems, unseen opportunities, or new and different ways to get the outcomes they want?

Things I will start doing or change...

CHAPTER 6
Building and Sustaining My Winning Team

Who are the winners, value creators, and solid building blocks on my team?

What am I doing that helps with the team's cohesiveness, communication, and esprit de corps?

Things I will keep doing...

CHAPTER 6
Building and Sustaining My Winning Team

Are there people or groups on my current team who are not sufficiently resilient, accountable, motivated to be the best, or able to create value or generally contribute positively to the team dynamic?

Things I will stop doing...

CHAPTER 6
Building and Sustaining My Winning Team

How can I change the team dynamic?

Are there aspects of team communication that I can positively affect?

Are there missing pieces that I need to somehow fill?

Things I will start doing or change...

CHAPTER 7
Building Our Coaching Culture

What current coaching activities do I regularly engage in with the team?

What about those coaching activities is going well?

Things I will keep doing...

CHAPTER 7
Building Our Coaching Culture

Which activities are supposed to feel like coaching to my team but turn out to be something different and less effective?

Which current coaching activities are having little, no, or a negative effect on the team's performance?

Things I will stop doing...

CHAPTER 7
Building Our Coaching Culture

How can we build upon the coaching culture we have currently?

How can we improve our cycle of planning together, observing people as they execute (e.g., in role-plays or in live action with customers), and offering constructive feedback?

What tools do we need to incorporate to support our coaching activities?

Things I will start doing or change...

CHAPTER 8
Leading My Team by Example

What do I do on a regular basis that serves as a proper and positive example of the behavior I want from my team?

What am I doing that solidifies what great looks like to them?

Things I will keep doing...

CHAPTER 8
Leading My Team by Example

What am I doing to set a less-than-excellent example for my team?

Have I been guilty of saying one thing but doing another? When? How can I avoid doing that again?

Things I will stop doing...

CHAPTER 8
Leading My Team by Example

What can I do to better exemplify the behavior that I want from my team?

Where might I need to lead the charge?

What other ways can I lead the team by example?

Things I will start doing or change...

CHAPTER 9
Establishing the Discipline of Planning

What aspects of planning with my team are going well and leading to positive results?

How can I preserve and protect the planning time we have together, preventing our discipline from eroding?

Things I will keep doing...

CHAPTER 9
Establishing the Discipline of Planning

What aspects of planning are we allowing to be overcome by events?

Are there any aspects of planning that we tend to forgo in favor of other activities?

What planning tools are we using that are not particularly helpful or are considered too onerous for the team and therefore an obstacle to planning?

Things I will stop doing...

CHAPTER 9
Establishing the Discipline of Planning

How can we improve our planning together at the account level, opportunity level, or call level?

How can we change and improve the tools we use to support planning?

How can I add more value to the process of planning for the team?

How can the team add more value to the process?

What changes do we need to make to our rhythm together to enable more time for planning?

Things I will start doing or change...

CHAPTER 10
Keeping My Team Motivated

What activities are having the most positive impact on team and individual levels of motivation?

Things I will keep doing...

CHAPTER 10
Keeping My Team Motivated

What activities or factors are currently demotivating the team?

Are there things that I do that sap the team's motivation?

Things I will stop doing...

CHAPTER 10
Keeping My Team Motivated

What can we do together to increase and sustain the degree to which the team is motivated to execute with excellence?

What can we do to encourage and incentivize the right behavior?

How can we increase the positivity factor of team meetings and activities?

Things I will start doing or change...

CHAPTER 11
Fine-Tuning the Team's Rhythm Together

What elements of our operating rhythm are going well and leading to positive outcomes?

Things I will keep doing...

CHAPTER 11
Fine-Tuning the Team's Rhythm Together

What aspects of our rhythm together seem to be time wasters or do not appear to have a direct impact on performance?

Things I will stop doing...

CHAPTER 11
Fine-Tuning the Team's Rhythm Together

How can we improve our rhythm together? What activities can we make more efficient, more effective, or both?

Things I will start doing or change...

Acknowledgments

For my partner in all things, my wife, Sandy: Thank you for making it possible for me to find time to write this book and for all that you do to hold our lives together. I couldn't do it without you!

For my parents, John and Irma McDarby, who taught me the value of hard work and for my siblings, Alice, John, Delia, and Anne, who live out the values that our father taught us every day — honesty, hard work, and having some fun along the way. This book is dedicated most of all to Dad's memory. I hope he would be proud.

To my parents-in-law, Rudy and Leta Falle, for being a fantastic support system for my wife and kids and allowing me to trust that they are in good hands whenever I had to be away.

For my friends, advisors, and my earliest supporter, Nancy Jillard, a woman of letters who offered a word of encouragement to a little boy who wasn't very sure of himself. Nancy: your words ring in my brain even now, and I pray your soul rests in peace.

Finally, for my children, Maggie, Clare, Thomas, and Colleen: This book is also dedicated to you. Remember every day that I require only three things of you: You must try your best, have fun, and learn something new. I am so very proud of each of you.

With regard to the production of this book, I want to acknowledge my editor and chief motivator on this project, Meredith Maslich; John Golden my friend, former boss, and very capable writer in his own right for his wonderful foreword; and to all of those featured in stories throughout this book, I owe my deepest thanks. Thank you to all of those who contributed in some small way to the completion of this book. This is a lifelong dream of mine, and I very much appreciate you being a part of the dream coming true.

About the Author

Matthew McDarby is a sales leadership coach and advisor to some of the world's best run sales forces, and he currently serves as Managing Director at Specialized Sales Systems.

In addition to leading his company's sales effort, he leads the company's research and advisory team. Prior to founding his own company, Matt served as the vice president of enterprise sales for Huthwaite, one of the world's leading sales training companies and creators of SPIN Selling. Before joining Huthwaite, he worked in sales, sales management, and consulting roles in the technology and professional services industries in the New York and Washington, D.C., metropolitan areas.

Matt has coached and advised hundreds of sales leaders and their salesforces in a wide range of industries, helping them win new business and create value for their clients. He has written or co-authored dozens of white papers, advisory briefs, and full length e-books on the subjects of sales excellence and sales leadership, and he frequently facilitates workshops to help salespeople gain a competitive edge in complex business-to-business sales.

Matt and his wife, Sandy, have four children and reside in the Washington, D.C., area. He is an active community, church, and youth sports volunteer, and he is a fanatical New York Giants fan.

Best ways to reach Matt:

Twitter	@mmcdarby
LinkedIn	www.linkedin.com/in/mattmcdarby
Company website	www.specializedsalessystems.com
Personal website	www.thecadenceofexcellence.com
Email	mmcdarby@specializedsalessystems.com

Printed in Great Britain
by Amazon